PRAYER AND RELIGION IN THE PUBLIC SCHOOLS

PRAYER AND RELIGION IN THE PUBLIC SCHOOLS

DAVID M. ACKERMAN, (EDITOR)

Novinka Books
New York, New York

Senior Editors: Susan Boriotti and Donna Dennis
Coordinating Editor: Tatiana Shohov
Office Manager: Annette Hellinger
Graphics: Wanda Serrano
Book Production: Matthew Kozlowski, Jonathan Rose and Jennifer Vogt
Circulation: Cathy DeGregory, Ave Maria Gonzalez, Raheem Miller and Andre Tillman
Communications and Acquisitions: Serge P. Shohov

Library of Congress Cataloging-in-Publication Data

LC Control Number: 2001058736

ISBN 1-59033-143-5.

Copyright © 2001 by Novinka Books
An Imprint of Nova Science Publishers, Inc.
227 Main Street, Suite 100
Huntington, New York 11743
Tele. 631-424-(NOVA) 6682   Fax 631-425-5933
E Mail Novascil@aol.com

All rights reserved. No part of this book may be reproduced, stored in a retrieval system or transmitted in any form or by any means: electronic, electrostatic, magnetic, tape, mechanical photocopying, recording or otherwise without permission from the publishers.

The authors and publisher have taken care in preparation of this book, but make no expressed or implied warranty of any kind and assume no responsibility for any errors or omissions. No liability is assumed for incidental or consequential damages in connection with or arising out of information contained in this book.

This publication is designed to provide accurate and authoritative information with regard to the subject matter covered herein. It is sold with the clear understanding that the publisher is not engaged in rendering legal or any other professional services. If legal or any other expert assistance is required, the services of a competent person should be sought. FROM A DECLARATION OF PARTICIPANTS JOINTLY ADOPTED BY A COMMITTEE OF THE AMERICAN BAR ASSOCIATION AND A COMMITTEE OF PUBLISHERS.

Printed in the United States of America

CONTENTS

Preface.. vii

Prayer and Religion in the Public Schools:
What is, and is Not, Permitted.. 1
    David M. Ackerman
    Summary 1
    Introduction 2
    Supreme Court Decisions 4
        (a) Devotional Exercises 4
        (b) Religious Instruction... 17
        (c) Private Religious Speech 21
        (d) Religious Objections to Curricular Requirements 25
    The Scope and Implications of the Decisions 26
        (a) What is Legally Permissible 26
        (b) What is Legally Prohibited 36
    Issues Not Yet Definitively Resolved 42
        (a) Religious Expression at Secondary School Commencement
            Ceremonies 43
        (b) Use of School Facilities After School Hours for Religious Worship
            46
    Conclusion 48

Bibliography 51

Author Index 75

Title Index 79

Subject Index 81

PREFACE

For whatever reason, Americans have always been fascinated by prayer and religion in their pubic schools. Since children spend a great deal of their productive hours each day in the school setting, the propagation or non-propagation of religious ideas is a legitimate issue. Many parents, especially those located outside the coastal elite states, believe that religious acts belong in schools as a crucial part of child-rearing. Those in the coastal states tend to support the absence of prayer in school, relegating it to the home as a matter of personal choice. The courts, by and large, have tended to support the minority and attempted to protect the rights of those who might be offended by public demonstrations of prayer, especially Christian reflections.

This book examines the core question of what is and what is not permitted regarding prayer and religion in the public schools as of the latest rulings and presents a selective bibliography of the book and journal literature for further analysis and reading.

PRAYER AND RELIGION IN THE PUBLIC SCHOOLS: WHAT IS, AND IS NOT, PERMITTED[1]

David M. Ackerman

SUMMARY

A recurring and politically volatile issue in constitutional law concerns the standards imposed by the religion and free speech clauses of the First Amendment on government involvement with religious activities and beliefs in the public schools. In pertinent part the First Amendment provides that "Congress shall make no law respecting an establishment of religion, or prohibiting the free exercise thereof; or abridging the freedom of speech..." Because each of these clauses is worded as an absolute, it is sometimes ambiguous whether governmental involvement in a given situation is a forbidden establishment of religion or a permissible or required accommodation of free exercise or speech. Nonetheless, the judicial interpretation of these clauses with respect to religious activities and expression in the public schools has been fairly consistent.

The Supreme Court has handed down eighteen rulings on various aspects of the matter, and the state and lower federal courts have added hundreds more. The gravamen of the courts' rulings has been that

---

[1] The author gratefully acknowledges the research assistance of intern Christopher Jennings in the preparation of this update.

government must be neutral regarding religion in the public schools, serving neither as its agent nor as its adversary. Religious expression that is genuinely private, in turn, has been held to be constitutionally protected.

Thus, the establishment clause has been held to bar government from using its authority or inculcate or proselytize about religious faith in the public schools, either directly or indirectly. Included in this proscription have been sponsorship of devotional exercises during the school day, at school events such as football games, and at secondary school graduation ceremonies; the adaptation of the school curriculum to particular religious dogmas; letting privately sponsored teachers come into the schoolrooms during the school day to give religious instruction; permitting only sectarian literature such as the Gideon Bible to be distributed by outside groups, and posting religious affirmations such as the Ten Commandments on classroom walls.

On the other hand, it has been held to be constitutionally permissible for government to give objective instruction about religion and religious literature as part of a secular program of education; to sponsor patriotic or ceremonial exercises which incidentally involve professions of faith; to accommodate private programs of religious instruction given off the public school premises; to permit student-initiated religious groups to meet in public school facilities during the school day on the same basis as non-religious student groups; to allow students to distribute religious literature; to permit religious expression in course work; and to exempt students with religious objections from particular attendance or curricular requirements. The courts have also affirmed the constitutionality of religious expression by students during the school day that is genuinely private and self-initiated.

This article summarizes each of the Supreme Court's decisions, gives a detailed overview of what has been held to be constitutionally permissible and constitutionally forbidden, and describes two issues as yet unsettled.

INTRODUCTION

Few issues in American public life have proven to be as persistent and as controversial as the issue of prayer and religion in the public schools. The issue has sparked political turmoil at least since the middle of the 19th century, and in recent decades it has spawned repeated battles in Congress, the state legislatures, the courts, political campaigns, and legal journals.

As a constitutional matter the issue primarily concerns the meaning and import of the religion and speech clauses of the First Amendment to the

Constitution providing that "Congress shall make no law respecting an establishment of religion, or prohibiting the free exercise thereof; or abridging the freedom of speech ...." Because these clauses are all worded as absolutes, it is often uncertain whether particular religious practices in the public schools should be deemed forms of private religious expression protected by the free exercise and/or free speech clauses or to be so infused with governmental action as to constitute a forbidden establishment of religion. The cases resound with complex questions of whether government's involvement with particular practices has a secular or religious purpose and effect, whether certain forms of expression constitute private religious speech, and whether certain facilities are the type of public for a from which religious expression cannot be excluded.

Particularly since the 1940s, when the Supreme Court first held the religion clauses to apply to the states as well as to the federal government,[2] the courts have been besieged with cases challenging the constitutionality of a variety of practices relating to religion in the public schools. The Supreme Court itself has handed down eighteen decisions on various aspects of the issue in the past four and a half decades, and the state and lower federal courts have handed down hundreds more. The practices that have been challenged have included regular devotional exercises such as prayer and Bible reading, the teaching of evolution and creationism, shared time and released time programs of religious instruction, meetings of student-initiated religious groups on school premises, the distribution of Gideon Bibles and other religious literature, the inclusion of prayers in commencement exercises and pre-game ceremonies at football games, compulsory recitations of the Pledge of Allegiance, prescribed moments of silence, the hanging of wall plaques containing religious affirmations, and restrictions on religious expression in course work.

Notwithstanding this plethora of judicial decisions and despite continuing political controversy over many of the rulings, the body of law that has developed has reflected a fairly consistent interpretation and

---

[2] The Fourteenth Amendment provides in pertinent part: "...nor shall any State deprive any person of life, liberty, or property, without due process of law.... In Cantwell v. Connecticut, 310 U.S. 296 (1941), and Everson v. Board of Education, 330 U.S. 1 (1947), the Court held the limitations imposed on the federal government by the free exercise and establishment clauses to be part of the "liberty" protected from undue State interference by the Fourteenth Amendment. The incorporation of the protections of the free speech clause had occurred earlier in Gitlow v. New York, 268 (U.S. 652 (1925).

application of the First Amendment. Not all of the issues can be said to have been judicially resolved, let alone politically accepted. But the courts' interpretation of the First Amendment with respect to prayer and religion in the public schools has been sufficiently consistent to permit a narrative overview. This report summarizes each of the pertinent Supreme Court decisions, gives a detailed overview of what the courts have held to be constitutionally permitted and proscribed, and identified and describes two issues that arguably still remain unsettled.[3]

SUPREME COURT DECISIONS

In eleven decisions the Supreme Court has held government **sponsorship** of, or **involvement** with, religious expression in the public schools to violate the establishment of religion clause. In seven other decisions, however, the Court has held government **accommodation** of religious activities or beliefs in the public schools to be constitutionally mandated or at least permissible. The following sections summarize each of these decisions under the rubrics of (a) devotional exercises, (b) religious instruction, (c) private religious speech, and (d) religious objections to curricular requirements.

(a) Devotional Exercises

(1) **Daily prayer and Bible reading.** In *Engel v. Vitale*[4] in 1962 and *Abington School District v. Schempp*[5] in 1963 the Supreme Court held the establishment of religious clause of the First Amendment to be violated by government sponsorship of daily devotional activities such as prayer and Bible reading in the public elementary and secondary schools. *Engel* involved a requirement of a local board of education in New York that students recite at the beginning of each school day a prayer that had been composed and recommended for use by the New York State Board of Regents:

---

[3] For a reprise of Congressional action on the issue, See CRS, *School Prayer.- Congressional Action, 1962-1998* (1998) (Report No. 96-846A).
[4] 370 U.S. 421 (1962).
[5] 374 U.S. 203 (1963).

> Almighty God, we acknowledge our dependence upon Thee, and we beg Thy blessings upon us, our parents, our teachers and our Country.

Abington (and the companion case of *Murray v. Curlett*[6]) concerned state requirements that each school day begin with readings from the Bible and the unison recital of the Lord's Prayer. In each case the states made provision for the excusal or nonparticipation of students at their request or the request of a parent or guardian.

Notwithstanding the excusal provisions, the Court, by a 6-1 majority in *Engel*[7] and an 8-1 majority in *Abington*,[8] held the exercises to be religious in nature and the states' sponsorship to violate the establishment of religion clause of the First Amendment. In *Engel* the Court asserted:

> (T)he constitutional prohibition against laws respecting an establishment of religion must at least mean that in this country it is no part of the business of government to compose official prayers for any group of the American people to recite as a part of a religious program carried on by government.
>
> ....
>
> (G)overnment in this country, be it state or federal, is without power to prescribe by law any particular form of prayer which is to be used as an official prayer in carrying on any program of governmentally sponsored religious activity.[9]

Similarly, in *Abington* the Court held:

> [The Bible-reading exercises] are religious exercises, required by the States in violation of the command of the First Amendment that the Government maintain strict neutrality, neither aiding nor opposing religion.[10]

---

[6] *Id.* This is the case that had been initiated by Madalyn Murray O'Hair.
[7] Justice Black authored the opinion of the Court in Engel, in which Chief Justice Warren and Justices Douglas, Clark, Harlan, and Brennan joined. Justice Douglas wrote a concurring opinion as well. Justice Stewart filed a dissenting opinion. Justices Frankfurter and White did not participate.
[8] Justice Clark authored the opinion of the Court in Abington, in which Chief Justice Warren and Justices Black, Douglas, Harlan, Brennan, White, and Goldberg joined. Justices Douglas, Brennan, and Goldberg each wrote a concurring opinion as well. Justice Stewart, as in Engel, submitted a dissenting opinion.
[9] Engel v. Vitale, *supra*, at 425 and 430.
[10] Abington School District v. Schempp, *supra*, at 203.

In both opinions the Court looked beyond the immediate words of the establishment clause to determine its meaning. In *Engel* it surveyed European and colonial history and identified two broad purposes underlying the establishment clause:

> Its first and most immediate purpose rested on the belief that a union of government and religion tends to destroy government and to degrade religion .... The Establishment Clause thus stands as an expression of principle on the part of the Founders of our Constitution that religion is too personal, too sacred, too holy, to permit its "unhallowed perversion" by a civil magistrate.[11]

The second purpose, the Court said, "rested upon an awareness of the historical fact that governmentally established religions and religious persecutions go hand in hand":

> It was in large part to get completely away from ... systematic religious persecution that the Founders brought into being our Nation, our Constitution, and our Bill of Rights with its prohibition against any governmental establishment of religion.[12]

In *Abington* the Court stressed that its previous decisions had "rejected unequivocally the contention that the Establishment Clause forbids only governmental preference of one religion over another."[13] Taken together with the free exercise clause, the Court stated, the establishment clause imposes on government a "wholesome neutrality" toward religion: It can neither favor one sect over all others, nor religion generally over non-religion, nor non-religion over religion. To be constitutional, the Court said, government action must be able to meet what subsequently became the *Lemon* test:

> The test may be stated as follows: What are the purpose and the primary effect of the enactment? It either is the advancement or inhibition of religion the enactment exceeds the scope of legislative power as circumscribed by the Constitution. That is to say that to withstand the strictures of the Establishment Clause

---

[11] Engel v. Vitale, *supra*, at 431-32.
[12] *Id.*, at 433.
[13] 375 U.S. at 216.

there must be a **secular legislative purpose** and a **primary effect that neither advances nor inhibits religion.**[14]

In both cases the Court rejected the argument that the "voluntary" nature of the prayer and Bible-reading exercises freed them from the strictures of the establishment clause.

> The Establishment Clause, unlike the Free Exercise Clause, does not depend upon any showing of direct governmental compulsion and is violated by the enactment of laws which establish an official religion whether those laws operate directly to coerce nonobserving individuals or not.[15]

It rejected as well the arguments that to deny states the power to prescribe religious activities in the public schools indicated hostility toward religion,[16]

---

[14] *Id.* at 222 (emphasis added). In most subsequent cases, the Court has continued to use the standards articulated by Justice Clark and has added a third aspect – whether the legislative enactment leads to excessive government entanglement with religion. Walz v. Tax Commission of the City of New York, 397 U.S. 664 (1970). Because the Court first gave the tripartite version of the test its full articulation in Lemon v. Kurtzman, 503 U.S. 602 (1971), the test has come to be known as the Lemon test. The Court has become sharply divided on the utility and applicability of the Lemon test, however; and as a consequence it is no longer the exclusive test the Court uses for establishment clause cases. The Court still uses the test; indeed, it used it in its most recent decision concerning prayer in the public schools. *See* Santa Fe Independent School District v. Doe, 120 S.Ct. 2266 (2000). But the Court also now uses the endorsement and coercion tests. In Agostini v. Felton, 521 U.S. 203 (1997), it might be noted, the Court modified the Lemon test by making the entanglement inquiry part of the inquiry into primary effect, at least for cases involving public aid to sectarian schools. Substantively, the entanglement inquiry appears to remain unchanged, and in any event the entanglement prong of the Lemon test has not often been a major factor in cases involving religious expression in the public schools.

[15] Engel v. Vitale, *supra*, at 421. In neither case did the Court actually make any finding with respect to whether participation in the exercises was in fact voluntary, holding that issue not to be material to its decisions. It suggested, however, that because of compulsory schooling, peer pressure, and the official sanction given the exercises, "voluntary" participation might be an impossibility. See Engel v. Vitale, *supra*, at 431 and Abington School District v. Schempp, *supra*, at 223.

[16] Justice Black in Engel noted that those who led the fight for religious freedom were themselves religious men and that the First Amendment grew out of "an awareness that governments of the past had shackled men's tongues to make

that the encroachments on the First Amendment made by state-prescribed prayer and Bible reading in the public schools were so minor and insignificant as to be *de minimis*,[17] and that not to allow the exercises denied the majority the free exercise of their religion.[18]

Justice Stewart dissented in both *Engel* and *Abington*. "With all respect," he said in *Engel*, "I think the Court has misapplied a great constitutional principle:

> I cannot see how an "official religion" is established by letting those who want to say a prayer say it. On the contrary, I think that to deny the wish of these school children to join in reciting this prayer is to deny them the opportunity of sharing in the spiritual heritage of our Nation.[19]

Citing numerous instances in which religious affirmations are made in public life, Justice Stewart rejected the majority's reliance on European and colonial history to give meaning to the establishment clause. "What is relevant," he said, "... [is] the history of the religious practices of our people, reflected in countless practices of the institutions and officials of our government."[20]

> them speak and to pray only to the God that government wanted them to pray to." Thus, he concluded:
>> It is neither sacrilegious nor antireligious to say that each separate government in this country should stay out of the business of writing or sanctioning official prayers and leave that purely religious function tot he people themselves and to those the people choose to look to for religious guidance.
>
> 370 U.S. at 421.

[17] Justice Clark said in Abington:
> The breach of neutrality that is today a trickling stream may all too soon become a raging torrent and, in the words of Madison, "it is proper to take alarm at the first experiment on our liberties."
>
> 375 U.S. at 225.

[18] Justice Clark stated in Abington:
> While the Free Exercise Clause clearly prohibits the use of state action to deny the rights of free exercise to anyone, it has never meant that a majority could use the machinery of the State to practice its beliefs.
>
> 374 U.S. at 226.

[19] Engel v. Vitale, *supra*, at 445 (Stewart, J., dissenting).
[20] *Id.* at 446.

Similarly, in *Abington* Justice Stewart contended that "the central value embodied in the First Amendment...is the safeguarding of an individual's right to free exercise of his religion..."[21]; and he suggested that the majority ignored that right in this case:

> ...[A] compulsory state educational system so structures a child's life that if religious exercises are held to be an impermissible activity in schools, religion is placed at an artificial and state-created disadvantage. Viewed in this light, permission of such exercises for those who want them is necessary if the schools are truly to be neutral in matters of religion. And a refusal to permit religious exercises thus is seen, not as the realization of state neutrality, but rather as the establishment of a religion of secularism, or at the least, as government support of the beliefs of those who think that religious exercises should be conducted only in private.[22]

Justice Stewart did not view the prayer and Bible reading exercises in *Abington* and *Murray* necessarily to be constitutional. The records, he said, were too thin to know; and consequently, he urged that the cases be remanded for further fact-finding. But the key question, he said, is whether government authority is used "to coerce a preference among [religious] beliefs." If the exercises were held before or after the official school day or were simply one among a number of "desirable" alternatives, he asserted, no one could claim that they "did anything more than to provide an opportunity for the voluntary expression of religious belief." On the other hand, he said, if there were no excusal provision or no alternative activities provided by school authorities, "the likelihood that children might be under at least some psychological compulsion to participate would be great."[23]

The Court's decisions in *Engle* and *Abington* spawned a variety of efforts in the states both to avoid and to defy the rulings. Subsequently, the Court has reviewed on the merits only three of the cases resulting from these efforts, but in each case it has reaffirmed the continuing vitality of *Engel* and *Abington*. In *Chamberlin v. Dade County Board of Public Instruction*[24] the

---

[21] Abington School District v. Schempp, *supra*, at 312.
[22] *Id*. at 313.
[23] *Id*. at 318.
[24] 143 So.2d 21 (Fla. 1962), *vacated and remanded*, 374 U.S. 487 (1963), *original opinion reinstated*, 160 So.2d 97 (Fla.), *reversed in part, dismissed in part*, 377 U.S. 402 (1964) (*per curiam*), *on remand*, 171 So.2d 535 (Fla. 1965).

Court reversed in a brief *per curiam* decision a Florida Supreme Court ruling which, in defiance of *Abington*, had held a state statute prescribing daily prayer and Bible reading to be constitutional. In *Karen B. v. Treen*[25] the Court summarily affirmed a lower federal court decision holding unconstitutional a Louisiana statute and a local school board's implementing regulation which permitted teachers to ask for student volunteers to offer a prayer at the beginning of each school day and, if no student volunteered, to offer a prayer themselves. Finally, in *Wallace v. Jaffree*[26] the Court summarily affirmed a lower federal court decision holding unconstitutional an Alabama statute which permitted teachers to lead students in prayer and set forth the text of a prayer to be recited.

In sum, then, the Supreme Court in *Engle* and *Abington* and in three subsequent summary decisions has held government sponsorship of daily devotional activities such as prayer and Bible reading in the public schools to constitute an establishment of religion and thus to be beyond government's constitutional power.

(2) **Commencement prayers.** In 1992 the Court in *Lee v. Weisman* held unconstitutional, 5-4, a public secondary school's inclusion of an invocation and benediction by a clergyman in its graduation ceremony.[27] In this instance the principal had decided that the prayers should be included, chosen a rabbi to deliver the prayers, directed that the prayers be nonsectarian, and instructed the students to stand as a group and maintain respectful silence

---

[25] 455 U.S. 913 (1982), *affg mem.* 653 F.2d 897 (5th Cir. 1981).

[26] 455 U.S. 924 (1984), *affg mem.* 705 F.23 1526 (11th Cir. 1983). The statute at issue in this cases provided as follows:

From henceforth, any teacher or professor in any public educational institution within the State of Alabama, recognizing that the Lord God is one, at the beginning of any homeroom or any class, may pray, may lad willing students in prayer, or may lead the willing students in the following prayer to God:
> Almighty God, You along are our God. We acknowledge You as the Creator and Supreme Judge of the world. May Your justice, Your trust and Your peace abound this day in the hearts of our countrymen, in the counsels of our government, in the sanctity of our homes and in the classrooms of our schools in the name of our Lord. Amen.

[27] Lee v. Weisman, 505 U.S. 577 (1992). Justice Kennedy authored the Court's opinion in Weisman, which was joined by Justices Blackmun, Stevens, O'Connor, and Souter. Justices Blackmun and Souter each filed concurring opinions as well, in each of which Justices Stevens and O'Connor joined. Justice Scalia issued a dissenting opinion, in which Chief Justice Rehnquist and Justices White and Thomas joined.

during the prayers. Explicitly reaffirming the school prayer decisions detailed in the preceding section, the Court said that

> the prayer exercises in this case are especially improper because the state has in every practical sense compelled attendance and participation in an explicit religious exercise at an event of singular importance to every student ....[28]

Reflecting its growing disenchantment with the *Lemon* test, the Court for the second time in its modern establishment clause jurisprudence chose not to use the test in analyzing the case.[29] Instead, the Court used the principle that "at a minimum the Constitution guarantees that government may not coerce anyone to support or participate in religion or its exercise." Noting that "prayer exercises in public schools carry a particular risk of indirect coercion," the Court concluded that in this instance "the State, in a school setting, in effect required participation in a religious exercise." Even though the prayer exercises were brief, the Court said, the intrusion on religious conscience "was both real and, in the context of a secondary school, a violation of the objectors' rights." "Government," it stated, "may no more use social pressure to enforce orthodoxy than it may use more direct means."[30]

The Court rejected the argument that students were not coerced into participating in a religious exercise because participation in the graduation ceremony was nominally voluntary: "Law reaches past formalism," it said, "and to say a teenage student has a real choice not to attend her high school graduation is formalistic in the extreme."[31] It rejected as well the argument that the nonsectarian or "civic" nature of the prayer exercises rendered them

---

[28] *Id.* at 598.
[29] The previous instance was March v. Chambers, 463 U.S. 783 (1983), in which the Court upheld as constitutional the offering of prayers by a chaplain at the opening of sessions of legislative bodies. Subsequently, the Court has also eschewed use of the Lemon test in Zobrest v. Catalina Foothills School District, 509 U.S. 1 (1993), Board of Education of the Kiryas Joel Village School District v. Grumet, 512 U.S. 687 (1994), and Rosenberger v. The Rector and Visitors of the University of Virginia, 515 U.S. 819 (1995). But it used the Lemon test in Lamb's Chapel v. Center Moriches Union Free School District, 508 U.S. 384 (1993), pointedly noting that *"Lemon* ... has not been overruled," Agostini V. Felton, 521 U.S. 203 (1997), Santa Fe Independent School District v. Doe, *supra*, and Mitchell v. Helms, 120 S.Ct. 2530 (2000).
[30] Lee v. Weisman, *supra*, at 594.
[31] *Id.* at 595.

unobjectionable, stating that "the design of the Constitution is that preservation and transmission of religious beliefs and worship is a responsibility and a choice committed to the private sphere, which itself is promised freedom to pursue that mission." Finally, the Court differentiated this case from the legislative chaplain's prayer held to be constitutional in *March v. Chambers, supra,* on the grounds that legislative prayer involves adults and that attendance is voluntary:

> The atmosphere at the opening of a session of a state legislature where adults are free to enter and leave with little comment and for any number of reasons cannot compare with the constraining potential of the one school event most important for the student to attend. The influence and force of a formal exercise in a school graduation are far greater than the prayer exercise we condoned in *Marsh* .... At a high school graduation, teachers and principals must and do retain a high degree of control over the precise contents of the program, the speeches, the timing, the movements, the dress, and the decorum of the students .... In this atmosphere the state-imposed character of an invocation and benediction by clergy selected by the school combine to make the prayer a state-sanctioned religious exercise in which the student was left with no alternative but to submit.[32]

The Court concluded:

> The sole question presented is whether a religious exercise may be conducted at a graduation ceremony in circumstances where, as we have found, young graduates who object are induced to conform. No holding by this Court suggests that a school can persuade or compel a student to participate in a religious exercise. That is being done here, and it is forbidden by the Establishment Clause of the First Amendment.[33]

Justice Scalia, joined by Chief Justice Rehnquist and Justices White and Thomas, dissented. Accusing the majority of "lay[ing] waste [to] a tradition that is as old as public school graduation ceremonies themselves, and that is a component of an even more longstanding American tradition of

---

[32] *Id.* at 597. For a fuller description of the distinctions the courts have drawn between school prayer and legislative prayer, *see CRS, Legislative prayer and School Prayer.- The Constitutional Difference* (1994) (Report No. 94-821 A).
[33] *Id.* at 599.

nonsectarian prayer to God at public celebrations generally," he charged that "the Court invents a boundless, and boundlessly manipulable, test of psychological coercion."[34] The establishment clause, he said, should be interpreted in light of American history; and "the history and tradition of our Nation," he asserted, "are replete with public ceremonies featuring prayers of thanksgiving and petition." Moreover, he stated, coercion ought to be construed to mean "by force of law and threat of penalty," not the majority's "ersatz, 'peer-pressure' psycho-coercion." Nothing in this case, he argued, compelled anyone to participate in a religious exercise.

(3) **Prayers at football games.** In *Santa Fe Independent School District v. Doe*[35] the Court held a school district's policy permitting students to vote on whether to have an "invocation and/or message" delivered prior to home football games by a student chosen for that purpose to violate the establishment clause, 6-3. Under the policy the high school student body would vote each spring whether to have an invocation or message during the pre-game ceremonies and, if they voted to do so, would choose who would deliver it from a list of student volunteers in another election. The student would then determine what invocation or message to deliver.

The Court held the policy on its face to violate each one of the tests it has formulated for establishment clause cases. The preference given for an "invocation" in the text of the policy, the long history of pre-game prayer led by a student "chaplain" in the school district, and the widespread perception that "the policy is about prayer," the Court said, made clear that the purpose of the prayer was not secular but was to preserve a popular state-sponsored religious practice in violation of the first prong of the *Lemon* test.

Moreover, it said, the policy violated the coercion test by forcing unwilling students into participating in a religious exercise. Some students – the cheerleaders, the band, the football players – had to attend, it said, and others were compelled by peer pressure to do so. "The constitutional command will not permit the District 'to exact religious conformity from a student as the price' of joining her classmates at a varsity football game,"[36] the Court held.

Finally, Justice Stevens wrote, the policy violated the endorsement test. The school district argued that the pre-game ceremonies constituted a public forum and that the election system guaranteed that the speech would be private student speech and not government-sponsored speech. But the Court

---

[34] *Id.* at 632 (Scalia, J., dissenting).
[35] Santa Fe Independent School District v. Doe, 120 S.Ct. 2266 (2000).

said that nothing evidenced any intention on the part of the school district to open the pre-game ceremonies for speech generally; and, it stated, in any event the election system violated the principle of viewpoint neutrality essential to such a forum, because it guaranteed that only majority views would prevail and that minority candidates and their views would be "effectively silenced." In addition, it held, the long history of pre-game prayer, the bias toward religion in the policy itself, the fact that the message would be "delivered to a large audience assembled as part of a regularly scheduled, school-sponsored function conducted on school property" and over the school's public address system all meant that the speech was not genuine private speech but would be perceived as "stamped with the school's seal of approval."

The Court concluded:

> The policy is invalid on its face because it establishes an improper majoritarian election on religion, and unquestionably has the purpose and creates the perception of encouraging the delivery of prayer at a series of important school events.[37]

Chief Justice Rehnquist, joined by Justices Scalia and Thomas, dissented, charging that the Court's ruling "bristles with hostility to all things religious in public life" and was wrong both procedurally and substantively. Procedurally, he argued, the Court should have waited for the policy to be implemented before ruling on its constitutionality so that there would be a record showing whether the elections were, in fact, about prayer. They might be, he said, but they might also focus on other factors; and the students, he stated, might even choose not to have a pre-game message. Substantively, he contended, the Court was wrong in saying that the policy was biased toward religion, that the student message would be public speech and not private speech, and that the history of pre-game prayer in the school district evidenced a purpose of continuing the practice. Solemnization, he argued, is not necessarily religious; the content of any message that would be delivered was wholly within the control of the student speaker; and the history of the policy showed that it was an effort to come into compliance with a court order. He concluded:

---

[36] *Id.* at 2280-81, quoting Lee v. Weisman, *supra*, at 596.
[37] *Id.* at 2283.

The policy at issue here may be applied in an unconstitutional manner, but it will be time enough to invalidate it if that is found to be the case.[38]

(4) Moments of silence. In *Wallace v. Jaffree* the Court held unconstitutional, 6-3, an Alabama statute prescribing that each day in both elementary and secondary school begin with a "period of silence ... for meditation or voluntary prayer."[39] The Court found that the Alabama Legislature adopted the statute in question in 1981 "for the sole purpose of expressing the State's endorsement of prayer activities for one minute at the beginning of each school day." Another statute previously adopted by Alabama in 1978, it noted, already provided for a moment of silence at the beginning of each school day for purposes of mediation. The legislative history of the addition of the phrase "or voluntary prayer" in the later statute, it concluded, clearly showed that the statute was intended to serve no secular purpose and was of a "wholly religious character."

The Court rebutted at length what it termed Alabama's "remarkable" contention that the establishment of religion clause bars only Congress and not the states from imposing an official religion:

> [I]t is ... appropriate to recall how firmly embedded in our constitutional jurisprudence is the proposition that the several States have no greater power to restrain the individual freedoms protected by the First Amendment than does the Congress of the United States....[W]hen the Constitution was amended to prohibit the States from depriving any person of liberty without due process of law, that Amendment imposed the same substantive limitations on the States' power to legislate that the First Amendment has always imposed on the Congress' power. This Court has confirmed and endorsed this elementary proposition of law time and time again.[40]

---

[38] *Id.* at 2288 (Rehnquist, C.J., dissenting).
[39] Wallace v. Jaffree, 472 U.S. 38 (1985). Justice Stevens authored the opinion of the Court, in which Justices Brennan, Marshall, Blackmun, and Powell joined. Justice O'Connor joined in the Court's judgment but authored a separate opinion setting forth her reasoning. Justice Powell also authored a concurring opinion. Chief Justice Burger and Justices White and Rehnquist each authored dissenting opinions.
[40] *Id.* at 48-49.

Finally, the Court stressed in *Wallace* that it was not holding all moment of silence provisions to be unconstitutional:

> The legislative intent to return prayer to the public schools is, of course, quite different from merely protecting every student's right to engage in voluntary prayer during an appropriate moment of silence during the schoolday. The 1978 statute already protected that right....[41]

Chief Justice Burger and Justices White and Rehnquist dissented. The Chief Justice contended that the mere addition of the word "prayer" to Alabama's silent medication statute as one of the permitted activities should not be taken as an endorsement of religion and that the majority misread the legislative history of the statute. Justice White agreed and called for "a basic reconsideration of our precedents." Justice Rehnquist penned an extensive critique of the metaphor "wall of separation between church and state, the *Lemon* test, and the history the Court had previously used to support its interpretation of the meaning of the establishment clause. He agreed that the states are prohibited by the incorporation of the First Amendment into the Fourteenth from establishing a religion. But, he said, "[a]s its history abundantly shows..., nothing in the Establishment Clause requires government to be strictly neutral between religion and irreligion, nor does that Clause prohibit Congress or the States from pursuing legitimate secular ends through nondiscriminatory sectarian means."[42] Even if the Alabama statute were understood to favor prayer, he contended, "[n]othing in the Establishment Clause of the First Amendment, properly understood, prohibits any such generalized 'endorsement' of prayer."[43]

---

[41] *Id.* at 59.

[42] *Id.* at 113 (Rehnquist, J., dissenting).

[43] *Id.* at 114. Not long after Wallace another moment of silence case came before the Court, this one involving a New Jersey statute prescribing a moment of silence "for quiet and private contemplation or introspection" that had been held unconstitutional by the lower courts. But the Court found that the parties who brought the appeal to it had no standing to do so, and as a consequence it did not reach the merits of the case. *See* May v. Cooperman, 572 F.Supp. 1561 (D. N.J. 1983), *aff'd*, 789 F.2d 240 (3d Cir. 1985), *appeal dism'd for want of jurisdiction*, 484 U.S. 72 (1987).

(b) Religious Instruction

(1) **Shared time programs.** In the 1948 case of *McCollum v. Board of Education* the Court held unconstitutional, 8-1, a "shared time" program in which the public schools permitted teachers employed by private religious groups to come into the schools each week to teach religion to consenting students.[44] The schools did not employ the teachers but cooperated closely with the program: the teachers were subject to the approval and supervision of the superintendent of schools; reports of students' attendance at the classes were made to the school; and non-participating students were required to go elsewhere in the school building. The Court held the program to constitute "a utilization of the tax-established and tax-supported public school system to aid religious groups to spread their faith." As such, the Court said, "... it falls squarely under the ban of the First amendment":

> (A) state cannot consistently with the First and Fourteenth Amendments utilize its public school system to aid any or all religious faiths or sects in the dissemination of their doctrines and ideals ....[45]

(2) **Released time programs.** Five years after the *McCollum* decision, the Court in *Zorach v. Clauson* upheld as constitutional a New York "released time" program of off-premises religious instruction, 6-3.[46] The program permitted public elementary and secondary school children so desiring to leave the school premises at a designated time during the school day to receive religious instruction from private teachers in nearby private facilities. The Court differentiated this program from that held unconstitutional in *McCollum* by stating:

---

[44] McCollum v. Board of Education, 333 U.S. 203 (1948). Justice Black authored the opinion of the Court in McCollum, in which Chief Justice Vinson and Justices Douglas, Murphy, Rutledge, and Burton joined. Justice Frankfurter authored a concurring opinion in which Justices Jackson, Rutledge, and Burton joined; and Justice Jackson authored a separate concurring opinion as well. Justice Reed dissented on the grounds that "well-recognized and long-established practices support the validity of the Illinois statute ...."

[45] *Id.* at 211.

[46] Zorach v. Clauson, 343 U.S. 306 (1952). Justice Douglas wrote the opinion of the Court, in which Chief Justice Vinson and Justices Reed, Burton, Clark, and Minton joined. Justices Black, Frankfurter, and Jackson filed dissenting opinions contending that there was no significant difference between the shared time struck down in McCollum and New York's released time program.

> In the *McCollum* case the classrooms were used for religious instruction and the force of the public school was used to promote that instruction. Here ... the public schools to no more than accommodate their schedules to a program of outside religious instruction.[47]

The First Amendment, the Court stated, forbids any "concert of union of dependency" between church and state, but it does not require that they "be aliens to each other – hostile, suspicious, and even unfriendly." In oft-quoted *dicta* Justice Douglas concluded for the Court:

> When the state encourages religious instruction or cooperates with religious authorities by adjusting the schedule of public events to sectarian needs, it follows the best of our traditions. For it then respects the religious nature of our people and accommodates the public service to their spiritual needs. Government may not finance religious groups nor undertake religious instruction nor blend secular and sectarian education nor use secular institutions to force one or some religion on any person.... But is can close its doors or suspend its operations as to those who want to repair to their religious sanctuary for worship or instruction. No more than that is undertaken here.[48]

(3) Evolution and creationism. In *Epperson v. Arkansas*[49] the Court unanimously held unconstitutional a state statute which forbade teachers upon pain of criminal penalty from teaching the Darwinian theory of evolution. The statute was a variant of the one involved in the famous Scopes trial in 1927[50] and made it unlawful for any teacher to teach or to use a textbook which taught "the theory or doctrine that mankind ascended or descended from a lower order of animals." The Court found that "fundamentalist sectarian conviction was and is the law's reason for existence," and because of that held the statute to violate the establishment

---

[47] *Id.* at 315.
[48] *Id.* at 313-14.
[49] Epperson v. Arkansas, 393 U.S. 97 (1968). Justice Fortas authored the opinion of the Court, in which Chief Justice Warren and Justices Douglas, Brennan, White, and Marshall joined. Justices Black, Harlan, and Stewart filed concurring opinions.
[50] Through Scopes' conviction was overturned on a technicality, the Tennessee Supreme Court held the statute itself to be constitutional. Scopes v. State, 154 Tenn. 105, 289 S.W. 263 (1927).

clause. Justice Fortas stated the general principled governing the case as follows:

> Government in our democracy, state and national, must be neutral in matters of religious theory, doctrine, and practice. It may not be hostile to any religion or to the advocacy of no-religion; and it may not aid, foster, or promote one religion or religious theory against the militant opposite. The First Amendment mandates governmental neutrality between religion and religion, and between religion and nonreligion.[51]

More particularly, he said, "the First Amendment does not permit the State to require that teaching and learning must be tailored to the principles or prohibitions of any religious sect of dogma.[52] In this instance, he stated,

> there can be no doubt that Arkansas has sought to prevent its teachers from discussing the theory of evolution because it is contrary to the belief of some that the Book of Genesis must be the exclusive source of doctrine as to the origin of man .... [T]here is no doubt that the motivation for the law was the same [as that in Tennessee's 'monkey law']: to suppress the teaching of a theory which, it was thought, 'denied' the divine creation of man.[53]

The state might have acted in a religiously neutral manner, the Court suggested, if it had simply excised from its curricula all discussion of the origins of mankind. But instead, it said, the state tried to blot out a particular theory because of its "supposed conflict" with "a particular religious group." That effort, the Court concluded, was "plainly" unconstitutional.

Two decades later in 1987 the Court reemphasized this reasoning in holding unconstitutional a Louisiana statute that required teachers to give "balanced treatment" to evolution and creationism if they taught the subject at all. In *Edwards v. Aguillard* the Court held, 7-2,[54] that in enacting the

---

[51] Epperson v. Arkansas, *supra*, at 103-04.
[52] Epperson v. Arkansas, *supra*, at 106.
[53] *Id*. at 107 and 109.
[54] Edwards v. Aguillard, 482 U.S. 578 (1987). Justice Brennan authored the opinion of the Court, in which Justices Marshall, Powell, Blackmun, Stevens, and O'Connor joined. Justice Powell, joined by Justice O'Connor, wrote a separate concurring opinion as well. Justice White concurred only in the Court's conclusion and authored a separate opinion detailing his reasoning. Justice

statute "the pre-eminent purpose of the Louisiana legislature was clearly to advance the religious viewpoint that a supernatural being created mankind."[55] Stating that it would not be "blind" to the "historic and contemporaneous antagonisms between the teachings of certain religious denominations and the teaching of evolution," the Court struck down the statute "because it seeks to employ the symbolic and financial support of government to achieve a religious purpose.[56] There was, Justice Brennan wrote for the Court, "no clear secular purpose" for the statute; the purposes stated in the Act, he said, were a "sham." The Act's purpose, he wrote, "was to restructure the science curriculum to conform with a particular religious viewpoint" and "to give preference to those religious groups which have as one of their tenets the creation of humankind by a divine creator." The Court concluded:

> [B]ecause the primary purpose of the Creationism Act is to endorse a particular religious doctrine, the Act furthers religion in violation of the Establishment Clause.[57]

(4) Posting of the Ten Commandments. In the fifth decision in this area, the Court in *Stone v. Graham* held unconstitutional, 5-4, a Kentucky statute which required that a copy of the Ten Commandments, purchased with private contributions, be posted on the wall of each public classroom in the state.[58] The Court, notwithstanding contrary declarations by the state legislature, found the "pre-eminent purpose" of the posting requirement to be "plainly religious in nature":

Scalia, joined by Chief Justice Rehnquist, filed a dissenting opinion arguing that the majority misread the statute's legislative history and that, in any event, courts should not lightly impugn the motives of legislators.

[55] *Id.* at 591.
[56] *Id.* at 597.
[57] *Id.* at 594.
[58] Stone v. Graham, 449 U.S. 39 (1980) (*per curiam*). Joining in the Court's *per curiam* opinion were Justices Brennan, White, Marshall, Powell, and Stevens. Chief Justice Burger and Justice Blackmun dissented on the procedural grounds that the Court should have, before making its decision in the case, received briefs and oral argument on the merits. Justices Stewart and Rehnquist dissented on the merits.

The Ten Commandments is undeniably a sacred text in the Jewish and Christian faiths, and no legislative recitation of a supposed secular purpose can blind us to that fact.[59]

As a consequence, the Court held that the "mere posting of the copies under the auspices of the legislature provide(d) the 'official support of the State...Government' that the Establishment Clause prohibits."

In sum, then, the Court in *McCollum, Zorach, Epperson, Aguillard,* and *Stone* held the establishment clause to bar government from using, or permitting private groups to use, the public schools to inculcate the tenets or beliefs of any religious faith.

(c) Private Religious Speech

(1) Noncurricular religious expression by students. In three decisions the Court has held that students at the secondary and/or college levels have a legal right to join together for purposes of noncurricular religious expression to the same extent as they may do so for nonreligious purposes. In *Widmar v. Vincent* the Court in 1981 held, 8-1, that a public university which permits student groups to use its facilities for secular purposes may not bar such groups from using the facilities for religious worship and discussion.[60] The Court based this holding not on the free exercise clause but on the free speech clause of the First Amendment. Saying that religious worship and discussion are forms of speech and association protected by the First Amendment, the Court asserted that once the University of Missouri-Kansas City opened its facilities for use by student organizations, it created a limited public forum. Consequently, it held, under the free speech clause the University could not discriminate in the kinds of speech it permitted unless it had a compelling reason for doing so.

The University argued that conformance with the establishment clause and with Missouri's history of strict church-state separation constituted sufficient justification for its ban. But the Court disagreed, saying the permitting student groups to use campus facilities for religious purposes

---

[59] *Id.* at 41.
[60] Widmar v. Vincent, 454 U.S. 263 (1981). Justice Powell wrote the opinion of the Court, in which Chief Justice Burger and Justices Brennan, Marshall, Balckmun, Rehnquist, and O'Connor joined. Justice Stevens filed a concurring opinion. Justice White dissented.

would neither place the imprimatur of University sponsorship on any sectarian belief or practice nor single out religious groups for special benefits. The Court concluded:

> Having a forum generally open to student groups, the University seeks to enforce a content-based exclusion of religious speech. Its exclusionary policy violates the fundamental principle that a state regulation of speech should be content-neutral, and the University is unable to justify this violation under applicable constitutional standards.[61]

In *Board of Education of Westside Community Schools v. Mergens* the Court, in an 8-1 decision, held constitutional a federal statute extending the *Widmar* principle to the secondary school level.[62] The statute at issue, the Equal Access Act,[63] was adopted in 1984 and bars public secondary schools that receive federal funds and that permit noncurriculum-related student groups to meet on school premises during noninstructional time from discriminating against any student group that wishes to meet on the basis of the religious, political, philosophical, or other content of the speech at such meetings. In *Mergens* the Court construed the Act broadly as a remedy against "perceived widespread discrimination against religious speech in public schools" and held it to apply any time a school permits even one

---

[61] *Id.* at 277.
[62] Board of Education of Westside Community Schools v. Mergens, 496 U.S. 226 (1990). Justice O'Connor wrote an opinion for the Court with respect to the construction of the Equal Access Act, in which Chief Justice Rehnquist and Justices White, Blackmun, Scalia, and Kennedy joined. She also authored a plurality opinion, in which Chief Justice Rehnquist and Justices White and Blackmun joined, upholding the constitutionality of the Act under the endorsement test (a reformulation of the Lemon test asking whether a government action intends to convey, or actually does convey, "a message that religion or a particular religious belief is favored or preferred"). Justice Kennedy, joined by Justice Scalia, authored an additional opinion also upholding the constitutionality of the Act but under the coercion test. Justice Marshall, joined by Justice Brennan, authored an opinion concurring in the judgment which agreed with the majority opinion on the construction of the Act and which also affirmed the constitutionality of the Act under the endorsement test, but only on the condition that Westside take several steps to more effectively disassociate itself from the religious clubs' speech. Justice Stevens dissented on the grounds the Act should be given a more narrow construction and that the Court failed to address the resulting establishment clause issues.
[63] 20 U.S.C.§§ 4071-74 (1988).

noncurriculum-related student group to meet. The Court further held that the extension of the subsidy to the student religious publication would not violate the establishment clause: Justice O'Connor asserted:

> There is a crucial difference between government speech endorsing religion, which the Establishment clause forbids, and private speech endorsing religion. We think that secondary school students are mature enough and are likely to understand that a school does not endorse or support student speech that it merely permits on a nondiscriminatory basis.[64]

Rosenberger v. Rector and Visitors of the University of Virginia raised another issue regarding student religious speech, namely, the constitutionality of excluding a student religious publication from a college program subsidizing the printing costs of all other student publications. The Court held the Constitution to mandate the religious publication's inclusion, 5-4.[65] The Court said that exclusion of the student religious publication from the subsidy program amounted to viewpoint discrimination in violation of the free speech clause of the First Amendment. "It is axiomatic," Justice Kennedy wrote, "that the government may not regulate speech based on its substantive content or the message it conveys." Once the government opens a limited public forum, he said, "it may not exclude speech where its distinction is not 'reasonable in light of the purpose served by the forum' ... nor may it discriminate against speech on the basis of its viewpoint." In this instance the University sought simply to "encourage a diversity of views from private speakers," he stated, and as a consequence the denial of the subsidy to the religious publication violated the students' right of free speech. The Court further held that the extension of the subsidy to the student religious publication would not violate the establishment clause:

> A central lesson of our decisions is that a significant factor in upholding governmental programs in the face of Establishment Clause attack is their neutrality toward religion .... We have held that the guarantee of neutrality is respected, not offended, when

---

[64] Board of Education v. Mergens, *supra*, at 250.
[65] Rosenberger v. Rector and Visitors of the University of Virginia, 515 U.S. 819 (1995). Justice Kennedy authored the opinion of the Court, in which Chief Justice Rehnquist and Justices O'Connor, Scalia, and Thomas joined. Justice Souter filed a dissenting opinion, in which Justices Stevens, Ginsburg, and Breyer joined.

the government, following neutral criteria and evenhanded policies, extends benefits to recipients whose ideologies and viewpoints, including religious ones, are broad and diverse.[66]

(2) **After-school use of premises by outside religious groups.** In *Lamb's Chapel v. Center Moriches Union Free School District* in 1993 the Court unanimously held unconstitutional a school district's refusal to permit a religious group to use school facilities to show a film series on family life.[67] The district generally permitted its facilities to be used for social, civic, and recreational purposes outside of school hours but it prohibited their use "by any group for religious purposes." Justice White, writing for the Court, concluded that the exclusion of religious groups was not viewpoint neutral and thus violated the free speech clause. "[I]t discriminated on the basis of viewpoint to permit school property to be used for the presentation of all views about family issues and child-rearing except those dealing with the subject matter from a religious viewpoint," he said. All other groups could use the facilities for lectures or film series about family values, he noted; only presentations from a religious perspective were banned.

The school argued that the establishment clause required it to exclude religious meetings, but the Court rejected the argument. There was "no realistic danger" in this instance, Justice White claimed, that "the community would think that the District was endorsing religion or any particular creed...." The film series would have been shown outside of school hours; it would not have been sponsored by the school; it would have been open to the public; and the facilities had been repeatedly used for similar purposes by a wide variety of private organizations. Under those conditions, he concluded, "any benefit to religion or to any particular creed would have been no more than incidental."

In sum, then, the Court in *Widmar* and *Mergens* held that students at the secondary school and college levels have a legal right to meet together in school facilities for religious purposes on the same basis as they may meet together for other noncurricular purposes. In *Rosenberger* it held that at the

---

[66] *Id.* at 834.
[67] Lamb's Chapel v. Center Moriches Union Free School District, 508 U.S. 384 (1993). Chief Justice Rehnquist and Justices Blackmun, Stevens, O'Connor, and Souter joined in Justice White's opinion for the Court. Justice Kennedy and Justice Scalia, joined by Justice Thomas, authored opinions concurring in the judgment of the Court but disagreeing with its reasoning on the establishment clause issue.

university level student religious publications must be treated the same as student nonreligious publications in any program subsidizing the expression of a diversity of viewpoints. Finally, in *Lamb's Chapel* it held that outside religious groups cannot be discriminated against in the after-school use of school facilities.

(d) Religious Objections to Curricular Requirements

In two decisions the Court has held the free exercise and free speech clauses to compel education authorities to honor religious objections to certain curricular requirements. The first case arose in the middle of World War II and confronted the Court with a conflict between a West Virginia requirement that all students join together each day in saluting the flag and reciting the Pledge of Allegiance and the religiously motivated refusal of students who were Jehovah's Witnesses to participate. The Court initially held the compulsory flag salute and pledge to be constitutional.[68] But in *West Virginia State Board of Education v. Barnette* the Court overturned that ruling and held, 6-3, that state compulsion of such affirmations of belief invades the realm of intellect and spirit protected by the First Amendment.[69] Resting the decision more on the free speech clause of the First Amendment than the free exercise clause, the Court asserted:

> Those who begin coercive elimination of dissent soon find themselves eliminating dissenters. Compulsory unification of opinion achieves only the unanimity of the graveyard. It seems trite, but necessary to say that the First Amendment to our Constitution was designed to avoid these ends by avoiding these beginnings.... If there is any fixed star in our constitutional constellation, it is that no official, high or petty, can prescribe what shall be orthodox in politics, nationalism, or religion, or other matters of opinion or force citizens to confess by word or act their faith therein.[70]

---

[68] Minersville School District v. Gobitis, 310 U.S. 586 (1940).
[69] West Virginia State Board of Education v. Barnette, 319 U.S. 624 (1943). Justice Jackson wrote the opinion of the Court, in which Chief Justice Stone and Justices Black, Douglas, Murphy, and Rutledge joined. Justices Roberts, Reed, and Frankfurter dissented.
[70] *Id.* at 641-42.

Thus, the Court held that government can sponsor patriotic ceremonies involving the flag salute and recitation of the Pledge of Allegiance in the schools but that it cannot compel students to participate.

In 1972 the Court in *Wisconsin v. Yoder* held, 6-1, that Wisconsin could not constitutionally compel Amish children to attend school beyond the eighth grade over the religious objections of their parents.[71] The Court noted that the Old Order Amish communities hold "a fundamental belief that salvation requires life in a church community separate and apart from the world and worldly influences" and that their religion dictates "devotion to a life in harmony with nature and the soil."[72] Although recognizing the importance of the state's duty to educate its citizens, the Court found that schooling beyond the eighth grade would "gravely endanger if not destroy" the Amish religion and way of life, and as a consequence held the free exercise clause to compel an exemption for them from the compulsory education requirement at the high school level.

In sum, the Court in *Barnette* and *Yoder* recognized, albeit to an indeterminate degree, a constitutional right of students and/or parents not to be compelled to participate in school programs or activities violative of their religious consciences.

THE SCOPE AND IMPLICATIONS OF THE DECISIONS

(a) What is Legally Permissible

The Supreme Court decisions summarized above, coupled with *dicta* in the Court's opinions and related state and lower federal court decisions, make clear that not all religious expression or government involvement with religion in the public schools is constitutionally forbidden. The Supreme Court and other courts have repeatedly affirmed, for instance, the constitutionality of government sponsorship of **objective** instruction about religion when it is done as part of a secular program of education in the

---

[71] Wisconsin v. Yoder, 406 U.S. 205 (1972). Chief Justice Burger wrote the opinion of the Court, in which Justices Brennan, Steward, White, Marshall, and Blackmun joined. Justices Stewart and White authored concurring opinions as well. Justice Douglas dissented. Justices Powell and Rehnquist took no part in the decision.
[72] *Id.* at 210.

public schools.[73] This principle has been held to extend to teaching about religious literature such as the Bible,[74] including religious perspectives in other courses,[75] recognizing and celebrating religious holidays,[76] and

---

[73] *Dicta* on this matter in Supreme Court decisions abound. In Engel, for instance, the Court noted:
> (I)t might well be said that one's education is not complete without a study of comparative religion or the history of religion and its relationship to the advancement of civilization. It certainly may be said that the Bible is worthy of study for its literary and historic qualities. Nothing we have said here indicates that such study of the Bible or of religion, when presented objectively as part of a secular program of education, may not be effected consistently with the First Amendment. 375 U.S. 203, 225.

In Epperson it reiterated:
> ... study of religion and of the Bible from a literary and historic viewpoint, presented objectively as part of a secular program of education, need not collide with the First Amendment's prohibition.... 393 U.S. 97, 106.

In Stone v. Graham the Court stated:
> this is not a case in which the Ten Commandments are integrated into the school curriculum, where the Bible may constitutionally be used in an appropriate study of history, civilization, ethics, comparative religion, or the like. 449 U.S. 39, 42.

[74] See *e.g.,* Wiley v. Franklin, 468 F. Supp. 133 (E.D. Tenn. 1979), *supplemental opinion,* 474 F. Supp. 525 (E.D. Tenn. 1979), *supplemental opinion,* 497 F. Supp. 390 (E.D. Tenn. 1980) (constitutionality of Bible as literature course upheld when taught by public teachers with bachelor's degrees in Biblical literature); Calvary Presbyterian Church v. University of Washington, 72 Wash.2d 912,435 P.2d 189 (1967), *cert. den.,* 393 U.S. 960 (1968) (constitutionality of public college-level course entitled "The Bible As Literature" affirmed); and Gibson v. Lee County School Board, 1 F.Supp.2d 1426 (M.D. Fla. 1998) (school's course on the Old Testament focusing on the temporal and cultural influences on its development held to be objective in nature and to be constitutional).

[75] Gheta v. Nassau County Community College, 33 F.Supp.2d 176 (D. Md. 1997) (community college course exploring the cultural and biological determinates of human sexuality that included a number of religious perspectives held not to promote religion and to be constitutional).

[76] See, *e.g.,* Florey v. Sioux Falls School District 49-6, 464 F. Supp. 911 (D. S. Dak. 1979), *aff'd,* 619 F.2d 1311 (8th Cir.), *cert. den.,* 449 U.S. 987 (1980) (local regulation permitting school observance of holidays having both a religious and secular basis upheld); Clever v. Cherry Hill Township Board of Education, 838 F.Supp. 929 (D. N.J. 1993) (school district policy requiring classrooms to maintain calendars depicting a variety of national, ethnic, and religious holidays and permitting seasonal displays containing religious symbols held not to violate the establishment clause); and Guyer v. School Board of Alachua County,

incorporating religious music in choral repertoires.[77] The Court also made clear in *Zorach* that a state can adopt "released" or "dismissed" time programs to accommodate those students who wish to leave the school grounds during the school day for private religious instruction elsewhere, and that holding has in no way been diminished by subsequent developments in the law.[78]

In addition, the courts have repeatedly affirmed the right of students to engage in private prayer or other religious expression individually or in groups during the school day, so long as the activity is not disruptive of the school environment and does not connote school endorsement of the activity.[79] Furthermore, *dicta* in the Court's opinion in *Wallace v. Jaffree*,

---

Florida, 634 So.2d 806 (1st Dist. Ct. App.), *cert. den.*, 513 U.S. 1044 (1994) (inclusion of symbols such as witches, cauldrons, and brooms in elementary school's Halloween festivities held not to violate establishment clause).

[77] Bauchman v. West High School, 132 F.3d 542 (10th Cir. 1997), *cert. Den.*, 524 U.S. 953 (1998) (music teacher's inclusion of explicitly Christian music in secondary school choir's concerts and selection of religious venues for performances held not to violate the establishment clause); Doe V. Duncanville Independent School District, 70 F.3d 402 (5th Cir. 1995) (inclusion of religious music in a high school choir's repertoire held not to endorse or advance religion and use of the song "The Lord Bless You and Keep You" as the choir theme song held not to constitute a forbidden religious exercise): and R.J.J. by Johnson v. Shineman, 668 S.W. 2d 910 (Mo. App. 1983) (inclusion of Christmas carols in concerts by high school chorus held not to alter fundamentally secular nature of concerts). *But see* Sease v. School District of Philadelphia, 811 F.Supp. 183 (E.D. Pa. 1993) (school's sponsorship, and school employee's leadership, or student Gospel Choir whose meetings and performances were "clearly religious in nature" held not to be protected activity under the Equal Access Act).

[78] Smith v. Smith, 523 F.2d 121 (4th Cir. 1975), *cert. Den.*, 423 U.S. 1073 (1976); State *ex rel.* Holt v. Thompson, 66 Wisc. 2d 659, 225 N.W.2d 678 (1975); Lanner v. Wimmer, 463 F. Supp. 867 (D.Utah 1978), *aff'd in part, rev'd in part*, 662 F.2d 1349 (10th Cir. 1981). *See also* Koenick v. Felton, 190 F.3d 259 (4th Cir. 1999) (closing of public schools on the Friday before, and the Monday after, Easter Sunday held not to have a primary effect of promoting religion but to be a permissible exercise of pragmatism and realism) and Bridenbaugh v. O'Bannon, 195 F.3d 796 (7th Cir. 1999) (statute designating Good Friday as a public holiday and closing state offices and public schools held not to promote religion but to serve the secular purposes of bolstering employee moral and giving all employees a long spring weekend).

[79] Santa Fe Independent School District v. Doe, 120 S.Ct. 2266 (2000) ("Nothing in the Constitution as interpreted by this Court prohibits any public school student from voluntarily praying at any time before, during, or after the schoolday"); Chandler v. James, 168 F.3d 806 (5th Cir. 1999), *vacated and remanded for reconsideration in light of Santa Fe Independent School District v. Doe, 120*

supra, suggest that there is no constitutional barrier to a state "protecting every student's right to engage in voluntary prayer" by providing for a moment of silence during the school day, so long as the government does not enact or administer such provision for the sole purpose of promoting prayer.[80]

Moreover, the First Amendment has been consistently interpreted to pose no bar to state sponsorship in the public schools of ceremonial or patriotic exercises which incidentally involve a profession of faith, such as the singing of the national anthem, the recitation of the Pledge of Allegiance, and the reading of such historical documents as the Declaration of Independence, so long as student participation is voluntary.[81] There also is

---

S.Ct. 2266 (2000) sub nom. Chandler v. Siegelman, 120 S.Ct. 2714 (2000) (lower court struck down part of an injunction requiring school officials to forbid students from participating in prayer or other devotional speech while at school or school-related events, holding that student religious expression at school events which is genuinely student-initiated does not violate the establishment clause and can be subjected only to the same time, place, and manner restrictions placed on secular speech in the schools); Chalifous v. New Caney Independent School District, 976 F.Supp. 659 (S.D. Tex.) (school policy prohibiting the wearing of gang-related attire and subsequent instruction that some students wear their rosaries inside their shirts held to violate their right of free exercise and not to be justified by any compelling school interest); and Redmon v. Clay County School Board, ___ F.Supp. ___ (M.D. Fla. 1992) (settlement permitted student to wear T-shirt with religious message to class).

[80] *See also* Abington, *supra*, at 280-81 (Brennan, J., concurring, stating that "even the observance of a moment of reverent silence at the opening of class" may serve the legitimate secular purposes of the devotional exercises struck down in that case "without jeopardizing either the religious liberties of any members of the community or the proper degree of separation between the spheres of religion and government"); Bown v. Gwinnet County School District, 895 F.Supp. 1564 (N.D. Ga. 1995), *aff'd*, 112 F.3d 1464 (11th Cir. 1997) (upholding the constitutionality of a Georgia statute mandating a "brief period of quiet reflection" at the beginning of each school day); Gaines v. Anderson, 421 F. Supp. 337 (D. Mass. 1976) (state statute prescribing a moment of silence at the beginning of each school day for purposes of "meditation or prayer" held constitutional); Opinion of the Justices, 113 N.H. 297, 307 A-2d 558 (1973) (advisory opinions affirming the constitutionality of proposed state statutes prescribing a period for silent meditation). *See also* Chaudhuri v. Tennessee, 130 F.3d 232 (7th Cir. 1997), *cert. Den.*, 523 U.S. 1024 (1998) (upholding the constitutionality of a state university's practice of having a moment of silence at graduation and other school events).

[81] In Engel the Court noted:
There is, of course, nothing in the decision reached here that is inconsistent with the fact that school children and others are

no constitutional barrier to the holding of baccalaureate services in conjunction with graduation ceremonies, at least so long as such services are privately sponsored and are not officially endorsed or promoted by the school system.[82]

---

    officially encouraged to express love for our country be reciting historical documents such as the Declaration of Independence which contain references to the Deity or by singing officially espouses anthems which include the composer's professions of faith in a Supreme Being, or with the fact that there are many manifestations in our public life of belief in God. Such patriotic or ceremonial occasions bear no true resemblance to the unquestioned religious exercise that the State of New York has sponsored in this instance.
    370 U.S. at 421 (ftnt. 21).
See also West Virginia State Board of Education v. Barnette, *supra* (imposition of penalty on student for refusal, for religious reasons, to join in recitation of Pledge of Allegiance held unconstitutional); Banks v. Board of Public Instruction of Date County, 450 F.2d 1103 (5th Cir. 1971) and Lipp v. Morris, 579 F.23 834 (3d Cir. 1978) (school board regulation and state statute requiring students not participating in salute and Pledge of Allegiance to the flag to stand quietly held unconstitutional); Smith v. Denny, 280 F. Supp. 651 (E.D. Cal. 1968), *appeal dism'd*, 417 F.2d 614 (9th Cir. 1969) (recitation of Pledge of Allegiance containing phrase "under God" held to be a patriotic ceremony rather than a religious exercise); Sherman v. Community Consolidated School District 21 of Wheeling Township, 980 F.2d 437 (7th Cir. 1992, *cert. Den.*, 508 U.S. 950 (1993) (state statute mandating the daily recitation of the Pledge of Allegiance in the public schools held to be constitutional so long as student participation is voluntary, and inclusion of phrase "under God" held to be a permissible ceremonial reference sanctioned by history); Sheldon v. Fannin, 221 F.Supp. 766 (D. Ariz. 1963) (singing of the national anthem in public schools held to be a patriotic rather than a religious 4exercise, but imposition of penalty on students refusing to take part for religious reasons held unconstitutional); and Opinion of the Justices, 372 Mass. 874, 363 N.E.2d 251 (1977) (state statute mandating that teachers and students recite the Pledge of Allegiance deemed to be unconstitutional because of element of compulsion).

[82] In a concurring opinion in Chamberlin v. Dade County Board of Public Instruction, *supra*, at 403, Justices Douglas and Black opined that baccalaureate services "do not present [a] substantial federal question." *See also* Goodwin v. Cross County School District No. 7, 394 F.Supp. 417 (E.D. Ark. 1973) (stipulation that baccalaureate services were held on school premises with minister as speaker held insufficient to establish their religious character); Verbena United Methodist Church v. Chilton County, 765 F.Supp 704 (M.D. Ala. 1991) (preliminary injunction issued ordering school board to allow private religious group to rent school auditorium for purpose of holding a baccalaureate service on condition that school officials take steps to disclaim any official connection to the event); and Randall v. Pegan, 765 F.Supp. 793 (W.D. N.Y. 1991) (rental

Moreover, in public colleges and universities student groups have been held to be constitutionally entitled to use campus facilities for religious worship and discussion to the same extent as other extracurricular student groups are permitted to use the facilities for secular purposes[83] and, under *Rosenberger*, to receive funding for their religious publications on the same basis as nonreligious student publications. At the public secondary school level students possess a legal right under the Equal Access Act analogous to *Widmar* to meet together for religious purposes during noncurricular time to the same extent as nonreligious student groups.[84] In addition, most courts

---

of school auditorium to stendent group for purposes of holding a baccalaureate service held not to violate the establishment clause).

[83] Widmar v. Vincent, *supra*.

[84] Board of Education of Westside Community Schools v. Mergens, *supra*. Prior to *Mergens* a number of courts had held the accommodation of student-initiated religious meetings on the premises of elementary or secondary schools not to be mandated by either the free exercise or free speech clauses of the First Amendment but, to the contrary, to violate the establishment clause. See Brandon v. Board of Education of the Guilderland Central School District, 635 F.2d 971 (2d Cir. 1980), *cert. Den.*, 454 U.S. 1123 (1981); Lubbock Civil Liberties Union v. Lubbock Independent School District, 669 F.2d 1038 (5th Cir. 1982), *cert. Den.*, 459 U.S. 1156 (1983); Bell v. Little Axe Independent School District, 766 F.2d 1391 (10th Cir. 1985); Garnett v. Renton School District No. 403, 874 F.2d 608 (9th Cir. 1989), *judgment vacated and case remanded for further consideration in light of Mergens*, 496 U.S. 914 (1990); Johnson v. Huntington Beach Union High School District, 137 Cal.Rptr. 43, 68 Cal.App.3d 1 (Ct. App.), *cert. Den.*, 434 U.S. 877 (1977); and Trietley v. Board of Education of the City of Buffalo, 65 A.D.2d 1, 409, N.Y.S. 2d 912 (App. Div. 1978). Indeed, prior to Mergens only one decision had applied the Supreme Court's reasoning in Widmar to student religious meetings at the secondary school level and held the free speech clause to compel accommodation of such a group. See Bender v. Williamsport Area School District, 563 F.Supp. 697 (M.D. Pa. 1983), *rev'd*, 741 F.2d 538 (3d Cir.), *vacated for want of jurisdiction*, 475 U.S. 534 (1986) (the Supreme Court held that the party that had taken an appeal from the district court's decision had no standing to do so, that therefore neither it nor the Third Circuit had jurisdiction to issue a decision in the case, and that, consequently, the district court's decision requiring that a student religious group be permitted to meet on school premises stood as the final decision in the case).

Litigation in the lower courts subsequent to *Mergens* has held the Equal Access Act to preempt state constitutional provisions that prohibit religious meetings on public property, to bar school personnel from playing an active role in student religious meetings, to be constitutional, and to override a school policy barring student groups from discriminating on grounds, *inter alia*, of religion in their selection of officers. See Garnett v. Renton School District, 987 F.2d 641 (9th

have upheld the right of students to distribute religious literature in the public schools on the same basis as other literature.[85]

Cir.), *cert. denied,* 510 U.S. 819 (1993) (Equal Access Act held to preempt contrary provision of Washington Constitution and to require school to allow students to form a religious club); Ceniceros v. Board of Trustees of the San Diego Unified School District, 106 F.3d 878 (9th Cir. 1997) (Equal Access Act held to preempt contrary provision of California Constitution and to require public secondary school to allow student religious groups to meet in an empty classroom during lunch on the same basis as other noncurriculum-related student groups); Hsu v. Roslyn Union Free School District, 85 F.3d 839 (2d Cir. 1996), *cert. den.,* 519 U.S. 1040 (1996) (provision in student religious group's charter stipulating that only Christians could be officers held to be protected by the Equal Access Act, notwithstanding school policy barring discrimination by student groups); and Hoppock v. Twin Falls School District No. 411, 772 F.Supp. 1160 (D Idaho 1991) (Equal Access Act held to preempt contrary provision of Idaho Constitution).

[85] *Compare* Hedges v. Wauconda Community Unit School District No. 118, 9 F3d 1295 (7th Cir. 1993) (School policies barring the distribution of all religious literature by students, or all religious literature which students might believe was endorsed by the school, held to violate free speech clause of the First Amendment but policies requiring fall literature to be distributed from a table near the front door and barring the distribution of more than 10 copies of material prepared by nonstudents upheld); Cintron v. State Board of Education, 384 F.Supp. 674 (D. P.R. 1974) (Commonwealth regulations barring the circulation of all religious literature in the public schools and recruitment within the schools for organizations with a religious/sectarian character, without any restriction to situations of disruption of the schools, held to be unconstitutionally vague and to violate the First Amendment's guarantees of a free press and free association); Thompson v. Waynesboro Area School District, 673 F.Supp. 1379 (M.D. Pa. 1987), *aff'd by an equally divided court,* No. 88-5235 (3d Cir., May 31, 1989) (school's refusal to permit junior high school students to distribute copies of their religious newspaper in school hallways held to violate students' free speech rights); Rivera v. East Otero School District R-1, 721 F. Supp. 1189 (D. Col. 1989) (school ban on the distribution of literature that "proselytizes a particular religious or political belief: held to violate students' rights of free speech); Slotterback v. Interboro School District, 766 F.Supp. 280 (E.D. Pa. 1991) (school district ban on distribution in the schools of materials that proselytize a particular religious or political belief held not to be justified either by the district's interest in providing an educational environment or in avoiding establishment clause problems and to be overbroad); Clark v. Dallas Independent School District, 806 F.Supp. 116 (N.D. Tex. 1992) (prohibition of students' distributing religious tracts held to be a violation of their free speech rights, absent any proof the restriction was necessary to avoid material and substantial interference with the operation of the school); Johnston-Loehner v. O'Brien, 859 F.Supp. 575 (M.D. Fla. 1994) (school policy requiring superintendent's approval for all written material to be distributed by students

Prayer and Religion in the Public Schools: What is, and is Not... 33

It is also clear that public schools at times are constitutionally **required** by the free exercise of religion clause of the First Amendment, and at other times constitutionally **permitted**, to accommodate their attendance and curricular requirements to the religious needs of their students and/or parents.[86]

---

held overbroad and unconstitutional); and Beach v. School Board of Leon County, No. 93-400048 (N.D. Fla. 1993) (settlement reached allowing 98th grader to distribute religious literature before and after school, between classes, and during lunch period) *with* Muller by Muller v. Jefferson Lighthouse School, 98 F.3d 1q530 (7th Cir. 1996), *cert. den.*, 520 U.S. 1156 (1997) (court held elementary school rules requiring the distribution of all nonschool materials to be approved beforehand and screened for offensive content not to be unconstitutional as applied to bar a 4th-grader from handing out invitations to a church meeting); Hernandez v. Hanson, 530 F. Supp. 1154 (D. Neb. 1977) (ban on distribution of religious literature held to be constitutionally permissible in order to avoid appearance of school endorsement of religious content of the literature); and Hemry by Hemry v. School Board of Colorado Springs, 760 F. Supp. 856 (D. Colo. 1991) (school policy barring the distribution of literature in school hallways held, as applied to students wanting to distribute religious literature, to be constitutional time, place, and manner restriction).

[86] Wisconsin v. Yoder, *supra* (Amish children held to be constitutionally entitled to exemption from State compulsory education requirement beyond the eighth grade). Other cases mandating or allowing state accommodation include Spence v. Bailey, 465 F.2d 797 (6th Cir. 1972) (denial of diploma to student who refused to take compulsory ROTC course for reasons of conscientious objection held unconstitutional); Moody v. Cronin, 484 F.Supp. 270 (C.D. Ill. 1979) (coeducational physical education requirement held unconstitutional with respect to children of Pentecostal parents religiously opposed to wearing 'immodest dress,' particularly in a coeducational setting); In the Matter of Alfonso v. Fernandez, 606 N.Y.S.2d 269 (1993) (program making condoms available in public high schools held to impose an impermissible burden on parents' due process right to direct their children's upbringing); Stark v. Independent School District, 123 F.2d 1068 (8th Cir. 1997), *cert. den.*, 523 U.S. 1094 (1998) (state approval of a charter school that eschewed use of television, radios, videos, and computers in accord with the founding parents' religious beliefs held not to violate the establishment clause); Chalifoux v. New Caney Independent School District, *supra* n. 63 (policy barring gang-related attire and requiring students to wear rosaries inside their shirts held to violate student's free exercise rights); and Hicks v. Halifax County Board of Education, 93 F.Supp.2d 649 (E.D. N.Car. 1999) (parent's challenge on religious grounds to school policy imposing uniform dress requirement on elementary school children without any opt-out provision for those with religious objections held to be subject to strict scrutiny under Yoder and defendant's motion for summary judgment denied). Cases in which accommodation was found not be be mandated include Mozert v. Hawkins County Public Schools, 827 F.2d 1058 (6th

The Supreme Court has also held that groups that offer a religious perspective on subjects otherwise permitted to be discussed in school facilities outside of school hours must be permitted to use the facilities.[87] Finally, several lower federal courts have affirmed that teachers have discretionary authority to allow religious expression in assigned course work.[88]

Cir. 1987), *cert. den.*, 484 U.S. 1066 (1988) (children of fundamentalist Christians offended by content of school system's reading curriculum held not to be entitled to exemption); Williams v. Board of Education of Kanawha County, 388 F.Supp. 93 (S.D. W.Va.), *aff'd mem.*, 530 F.2d 971 (4th Cir. 1975) (parents' challenge to textbooks and supplementary materials in public schools as anti-religious and offensive to Christian morals dismissed); Grove v. Mead School District No. 354, 753 F.2d 1528 (9th Cir. 1985), *cert. den.*, 474 U.S. 826 (1986) (parent's religious objection to use of Gordon Parks' *The Learning Tree* in a high school English class denied where her daughter had been given a different book to read and the option of leaving the classroom during discussions of the book); Brown v. Hot, Sexy and Safer Productions, Inc., 68 F.3d 525 (1st Cir, 1995), *cert. den.*, 516 U.S. 1159 (1996) (school requirement that students attend AIDS and sex education classes held not to violate free exercise clause or parents' right to direct their children's upbringing); Curtis v. School Committee of Falmouth, 420 Mass. 749, 652 N.E. 2d 580 (1995), *cert. den.*, 516 U.S. 1067 (1996) (public school program making condoms available to secondary school students without parental consent or an opt-out feature held not to violate free exercise or parents' rights); and Triplett v. Livingston County Board of Education, 967 S.W.2d 25 (Ky. Ct. App. 1997) (requirement that all students take a standardized examination held to violate neither the establishment clause nor the free exercise clause, notwithstanding parents' claims that test invaded their religious and moral beliefs and forced students to select morally objectionable responses).

[87] Lamb's Chapel v. Center Moriches Union Free School District, *supra*.

[88] *See* Settle v. Dickson County School Board, 52 F.3d 152 (6th Cir.), *cert. den.*, 516 U.S. 989 (1995) (grade of zero on research paper assignment to ninth grader who refused to do a paper on a subject other than Jesus Christ upheld as within the teacher's "broad discretion...in administering the curriculum"); DeNooyer v. Livonia Public Schools, 799 F.Supp. 744 (E.D. Mich. 1992), *aff'd without published opinion sub nom* DeNooyer v. Merinell, 1 F.3d 1240 and 12 F.3d 211 (6th Cir. 1993), *cert. den.*, 511 U.S. 1031 (1994) (second grade teacher held to have "legitimate pedagogical interests" in refusing to permit a child to show a video of herself singing a proselytizing religious song during show and tell time); and Duran by and through Duran v. Nitsche, 780 F.Supp. 1048 (E.D. Pa. 1991), *vacated and appeal dismissed*, 972 F.2d 1331 (3d Cir. 1992) (fifth grade teacher's refusal to permit a student to distribute a survey on religious beliefs as part of an independent study project and subsequent requirement, after he failed to make any progress reports to her, that he give his final oral report on the

Thus, the courts have construed the religion and speech clauses of the First Amendment to give government considerable room to teach about religion and to accommodate incidental and private religious expression in the public schools. Litigation in this area of the law is necessarily fact-specific. But in general judicial interpretations of the First Amendment have held that there is no constitutional or other legal barrier at the federal level to government

- providing objective instruction about religion in the public schools, including religious literature, holidays, and music;
- releasing students during the school day to receive religious instruction off the school premises;
- accommodating non-disruptive religious speech and the distribution of religious literature by students;
- permitting student-initiated religious groups to meet in school facilities for religious purposes;
- sponsoring noncompulsory patriotic or ceremonial exercises that involve incidental professions of faith;
- legislating moments of silence for meditation or reflection;
- exempting students with religious objections from particular course requirements;
- renting school facilities to private religious groups for the purpose of baccalaureate services or other meetings on the same basis as rentals to non-religious groups; and

---

project to her alone rather than to the class held to be "reasonably related to legitimate pedagogical concerns").
These cases seem in accord with the general principles the Supreme Court has articulated. The Court has made clear that "students ... do not shed their constitutional rights to freedom of speech or expression at the schoolhouse gate." But is has also made clear that "the constitutional rights of students in public schools are not automatically coextensive with the rights of adults in other settings." The general standard appears to be that
    educators do not offend the First Amendment by exercising editorial control over the style and content of student speech in school-sponsored expressive activities so long as their actions are reasonably related to legitimate pedagogical concerns.
See Tinker v. Des Moines Independent Community School District, 393 U.S. 503, 506 (1969); Bethel School District No. 43 v. Fraser, 478 U.S. 675, 682 (1986); and Hazelwood School District v. Kuhimeier, 484 U.S. 260 (1988), respectively.

- allowing religious expression in student course work where pedagogically appropriate.

(b) What is Legally Prohibited

Nonetheless, the scope of the limitations imposed by the establishment clause of the First Amendment remains broad: Government is constitutionally barred from using the public schools directly or indirectly to inculcate religious faith or belief.

Thus, government has been held to be legally prohibited from sponsoring or prescribing regular devotional exercises such as prayer and Bible reading in the public schools. This proscription has been held to apply to organized devotional exercises done pursuant to statute, school board regulation, school directive, and principal/teacher initiative or approval; to apply regardless of whether student participation is mandatory or voluntary; and to apply to devotional activities before or during a school's opening exercises, in the classroom, at school assemblies, and over the intercom.[89]

---

[89] State and lower federal court cases subsequent to the Supreme Court decisions in Engel and Abington have involved forms of state sponsored prayer and/or Bible reading identical to those in Engel and Abington as well as a number of variants. All have been found unconstitutional. *See, e.g.,* Alabama Civil Liberties Union v. Wallace 331 F. Supp. 966 (M.D. Ala. 1971), *aff'd*, 456 F.2d 1069 (5th Cir. 1972) (state statute prescribing daily Bible reading held unconstitutional); Kent v. Commissioner of Education, 402 N.E.2d 1340 (Mass. 1980) (state statute providing for daily period of prayer by student volunteer held unconstitutional); DeSpain v. DeKalb County School District, 225 F. Supp. 655 (N.D. Ill. 1966), *reversed*, 384 F.23 936 (7th Cir. 1967), *cert. den.*, 390 U.S. 906 (1968) (teacher sponsorship of pre-snack verse of thanks by kindergarten children held unconstitutional); State Board of Education v. Board of Education of Netcong, New Jersey, 108 J.J. Sup. 564, 262 A.2d 21, *aff'd*, 57 N.J. 172, 270 A.2d 412 (1970), *cert. den.*, 401 U.S. 1013 (1971) (school board sponsorship of daily "free exercise of religion: period during which students read aloud the chaplain's prayers from the *Congressional Record* held unconstitutional), Collins v. Chandler United School District, 470 F. Supp. 959 (D. Ariz. 1979), *aff'd*, 644 F.2d 759 (9th Cir.), *cert. den.*, 454 U.S. 863 (1981) (student council sponsorship of prayer by students at beginning of school assemblies held unconstitutional); Steele v. Van Buren Public Schools, 845 F.2d 1492 (8th Cir. 1988) (band leader's policy of beginning rehearsals and performances with prayer held unconstitutional); Douglas County School District v. Jager, 862 F.2d 824 (11h Cir.), *cert. den.*, 490 U.S. 1090 (1989) (delivery of invocations by clergy prior to public high school's football games held to violate establishment

Prayer and Religion in the Public Schools: What is, and is Not... 37

The proscription of governmentally sponsored prayer has also been held to extend to school-sponsored prayers by a clergyman at a public secondary school commencement exercise[90] and to prayers at athletic contests led by students elected for that purpose.[91] Finally, the proscription has been held to extend to provisions mandating or allowing moments of silence in the public schools where the provisions have been enacted for the exclusively religious purpose of promoting prayer.[92]

---

clause); Ingebretson v. Jackson Public School District, 88 F.3d 274 (5th Cir. 1996), *cert. den. sub nom* Moore v. Ingebretsen, 519 U.S. 968 (1996) (Mississippi statute permitting students to offer "nonsectarian, nonproselytizing ... voluntary prayer" at compulsory and noncompulsory school events held unconstitutional); Herdahl v. Pontotoc County School District, *supra* (prayers by a student club over the intercom each morning and vocal group prayers in elementary school classrooms prior to lunch each day held unconstitutional); and Committee for Voluntary Prayer v. Wimberly, 704 A.2d 1199 (D.D.C. 1997) (proposed ballot initiative to allow nonsectarian, non-proselytizing, student-initiated prayer at student assemblies, sporting events, graduation ceremonies, and other school-related events held unconstitutional). *Cf.* Coles v. Cleveland Board of Education, 171 F.3d 369 (6th Cir. 1999) (school board's practice of opening sessions with prayer led by local religious leaders or the school board president held to violate the establishment clause). *But see* Bacus v. Palo Verde Unified School District Board of Education, 11 F.Supp.2d 1192 (C.D. Cal. 1998) (school board's practice of opening sessions with prayers led by persons invited by the school board president upheld as constitutional).

[90] Lee v. Weisman, *supra*.

[91] Santa Fe Independent School District v. Doe, *supra*; Doe v. Duncanville Independent School District, 70 F.3d 402 (5th Cir. 1994) (prayers initiated by coaches during physical education classes, at pep rallies, and at athletic contests, held unconstitutional); and Doe v. Aldine Independent School District, 563 F.Supp. 883 (S.D. Tex. 1982) (posting and use of a school prayer at athletic contests and pep rallies held unconstitutional).

[92] Wallace v. Jaffree, *supra*; May v. Cooperman, *supra*; Beck v. McElrath, 548 F. Supp. 1161 (M.D. Tenn. 1982), *vacated as moot sub nom.* Beck v. Alexander, 718 F.2d 1098 (6th Cir. 1983) (state statute prescribing moment of silence for "meditation or prayer or personal beliefs" fouond to have been adopted for religious prupose and thus to be unconstitutional); Duffy v. Las Cruces Public Schools, 557 F.Supp. 1013 (D. N.M. 1983), *appeal dism'd*, No. CA 83-1358 (10th Cir. July 7, 1983) (state statute and local school board regulations permitting moment of silence in public schools for "contemplation, meditation or prayer" held to have religious purpose and effect and thus to be unconstitutional), Walter v. West Virginia Board of Education, 610 F.Supp. 1169 (D. W.Va. 1985) (constitutional amendment adopted by referendum providing for "brief time at the beginning of each school day for any student to exercise their right to personal and private contemplation, medication, or prayer"

In addition, the establishment clause has been consistently construed to bar government from itself teaching or inculcating the precepts or prohibitions of any particular sect or dogma in the school curriculum[93] and,

---

held to have a purpose of returning prayer to the public schools and to be unconstitutional).

[93] Epperson v. Arkansas, *supra*, and Edwards v. Aguillard, *supra*. Other cases concerning evolution include Webster v. New Lenox School District No. 122, 917 F.2d 1004 (7th Cir. 1990) (school district prohibition against teaching of creation science upheld); McLean v. Arkansas Board of Education, 529 F.Supp. 1255 (E.D. Ark. 1982) (state Statute prescribing equal time for evolutionary and creationist perspectives in public school curriculum held unconstitutional); Peloza v. Capistrano Unified School District, 37 F.3d 517 (9th Cir. 1994), *cert. den.*, 515 U.S. 1173 (1995) (school district directive requiring biology teacher to teach theory of evolution and prohibiting teaching of creationism and discussion of religious views outside the classroom during school hours upheld); and Freiler V. Tangipahoa Parish, Louisiana Board of Education, 185 F.3d 337 (5th Cir.), *cert. den.*, 120 S.Ct. 2706 (2000) (school board requirement that teachers read a disclaimer prior to any presentations on the theory of evolution stating that the purpose was to inform students of a scientific concept and not to influence their beliefs regarding the Biblical story of creation held to violate the establishment clause).

Other cases concerning religion in the curriculum include Hall v. Board of School Commissioners of Conecuh County, Alabama, 656 F.2d 999 (5th Cir. 1981) (high school course in Bible Literature found to have primary effect of advancing fundamentalist Christianity and thus to be unconstitutional); Lanner v. Wimmer, 463 F.Supp. 867 (D. Utah 1978), *aff'd in part, rev'd in part*, 662 F.2d 1349 (10th Cir. 1981) (public school course credit for Bible history courses taught in nearby Mormon seminaries held barred by First Amendment); Klein v. Kenton County School District, No. 89-164 (E.D. Ky. Dec. 18, 1989) (Bible study course in elementary school curriculum held to be unconstitutional); Herdahl v. Pontotoc County School District, 933 F.Supp. 582 (N.D. Miss. 1996) (course on "The Biblical History of the Middle East" found to espouse Christian fundamentalist views to students and thus to be unconstitutional); Marchi v. Board of Cooperative Educational Services of Albany, Schoharie, Schenectady, and Saratoga Counties, 173 F.23 469 (2d Cir. 1999) (school board's order to recently converted high school special education teacher to cease teaching about forgiveness, reconciliation, and God upheld as constitutional because of the board's strong interest in avoiding an establishment clause violation; Edwards v. California University of Pennsylvania, 156 F.3d 488 (3d Cir. 1998), *cert. den.*, 525 U.S. 1143 (1999) (reproof of education professor for including didactic religious materials in his courses on educational media and tests and restriction of his curriculum outline and the materials he could use held to be within the university's right to fix the curriculum); Gibson v. Lee County School Board, 1 F.Supp. 2d 1426 (M.D. Fla. 1998) (school's course on the New Testament that included Jesus' resurrection held to be religious in nature and to be unconstitutional); and Altman v. Bedford Central School District, 45 F.Supp.2d

more generally, from using its authority to promote religion.[94] Government has also been held to be constitutionally barred from permitting private parties to use the public school premises for the purpose of giving religious instruction to consenting students during the school day (shared time programs).[95]

---

368 (S.D. N.Y. 1999) (school's inclusion of prayers to the earth and a liturgy on Earth Day, suggestions that Worry Dolls had occult powers, and having students make a model of a Hindu god held to violate First Amendment). *Cf* Smith v. Board of School Commissioners of Mobile County, 827 F.2d 684 (11th Cir. 1987) (history and home economics textbooks recommended for use in Alabama's schools held neither to promote secular humanism nor to denigrate theistic religion); Brown v. Woodland Joint Unified School District, 27 F.3d 1373 (9th Cir. 1994) (inclusion of 32 stories and activities involving witches and witchcraft out of 10,000 stories/activities in the *Impressions* curriculum held not to violate establishment clause); and Fleishfresser v. Director of School District 200, 16 F.3d 680 (7th Cir. 1994) (*Impressions* curriculum held not to teach religious belief in supernatural beings in violation of establishment clause or to violate parents' free exercise rights).

[94] Roberts v. Madigan, 921 F.2d 1047 (10th Cir. 1990), *cert. den.*, 505 U.S. 1218 (1992) (school prohibition of teacher's display and reading of Bible during silent reading periods and of religious wall poster in his classroom upheld); Bishop v. Aronov, 926 F.2d 1066 (11th Cir.), *cert. den. sub nom.* Bishop v. Delchamps, 505 U.S. 1218 (1992) (public university's memorandum to professor directing him to cease interjecting his religious beliefs into classroom discussions and holding optional classes giving a Christian perspective of his subject matter upheld); Doe v. Beaumont School District, 173 F.3d 275 (5th Cir. 1999) (school district's use only of clergy in providing counseling to students during school hours held to violate the establishment clause); Peloza v. Capistrano Unified School District, *supra* (school district directive barring biology teacher from discussing his religious view with students upheld); and Smith v. Blue Valley Unified School District, No. 87-2415-0, 1989 U.S. Dist. LEXIS 4067 (D. Kan. April 24, 1989) (termination of assistant principal for refusal to stop discussions with students about religious subjects upheld). *But see* Clayton v. Place, 884 F.2d 376 (8th Cir. 1989), *cert. den.*, 494 U.S. 1081 (1990) (school board ban on dancing in the public schools held constitutional notwithstanding that its adoption was due to an aggressive campaign by religious group).

[95] McCollum v. Board of Education, *supra*; Malnak v. Yogi, 440 F.Supp. 1284 (D. N.J. 1988), *aff'd*, 592 F.2d 197 (3d Cir. 1979) (course in Transcendental Meditation taught by members of the World Plan Executive Council–United States held to be religious in nature and state sponsorship in high schools, as a consequence, to be unconstitutional); Wiley v. Franklin, *supra* (Bible study course taught and funded by private religious group in the public schools held unconstitutional); Doe v. Human, 725 F.Supp. 1503 (W.D. Ark. 1989), *aff'd*, 923 F.2d 857 (8th Cir. 1990); *cert. den.*, 449 U.S. 922 (1991) (school district enjoined from permitting outside teachers to come into the school to give Bible

The establishment clause has also been held to bar government from posting religious texts such as the Ten Commandments on classroom walls[96] and from permanently displaying religious paintings on school property.[97] The courts have further generally held the public elementary and secondary schools to be constitutionally barred from allowing only religious literature such as the Gideon Bible to be distributed by outside groups to consenting school children.[98] And the courts have found no constitutional violation in state statutes forbidding teachers from wearing religious attire.[99]

---

instruction during school hours); Doe v. Shenandoah County School Board, 737 F.Supp. 913 (W.D. Va. 1990) (school district barred from permitting Weekday Religious Education, Inc., from parking its remodeled school buses on school property next to public school and from encouraging students to take part in its religious education classes); Quappe v. Endry, 772 F.Supp. 1004 (S.D. Ohio 1991) (requirement that Bible club involving adults and 5th and 6th graders meet on school premises in the evening rather than immediately after school held to be required by the establishment clause); Herdahl v. Pontotoc County School District, *supra* (course on "The Biblical History of the Middle East" taught from a fundamentalist Christian perspective by outside teachers held to be unconstitutional).

[96] Stone v. Graham, *supra*. See also Doe v. Harlan County School District, 96 F.Supp. 2d 667 (E.D. Ky. 2000) (school board policy requiring the posting of the Ten Commandments in every classroom held to violate the establishment clause, and modification of policy after suit was filed to include various other historical documents held to be pretextual and not to cure constitutional violation); DiLoreto v. Board of Education of Downey United School District, 196 F.3d 958 (9t^{h} Cir. 1999), *cert. den.*, 120 D.Ct. 1674 (2000) (public high school's refusal to post an ad listing the Ten Commandments on a baseball field fence it had made available for commercial advertising held not to violate free speech clause of the First Amendment on grounds the fence was a nonpublic forum and the school had a reasonable concern that the ad would create disruption and controversy); and DiLoreto v. Board of Education of Downey United School District, 74 Cal.App.4th 267, 87 Cal.Rptr.2d 791 (Ct. App. 2d Dist. 1999) (same issue but ruling that the posting would have violated the establishment clause of the California Constitution).

[97] Washegesic v. Bloomingdale Public Schools, 33 F.3d 679 (6th Cir. 1994), *cert. den.*, 514 U.S. 1095 (1995) (school display of print of Warner Sallman's *Head of Christ* in main hallway for more than three decades held to promote religion and thus to violate the establishment clause) and Joki v. Schuylerville Central School District, 745 F.Supp. 823 (W.D. N.Y. 1990) (school's display since 1965 of large painting of crucifixion of Jesus in school auditorium held unconstitutional).

[98] Tudor v. Board of Education of Borough of Rutherford, 14 N.J. 31, 100 A.2d 857 (1943), *cert. den.*, 348 U.S. 816 (1955); Brown v. Orange County Board of Public Instruction, 128 So.2d 181 (Fla. App. 1960), *aff'd*, 155 So.2d 371 (Fla. 1963); Goodwin v. Cross County School District No. 7, 394 F. Supp. 417 (E.D.

Finally, government has been held to be constitutionally disabled from compelling students to participate in patriotic or ceremonial rituals involving affirmations of belief[100] and, to an undefined extent, from imposing curricular requirements that coerce students to violate their religious beliefs.[101]

Ark. 1973); Meltzer v. Board of Public Instruction of Orange County, Florida, 548 F.2d 599 (5th Cir. 1988), *on rehearing en banc*, 577 F.23 211 (5th Cir. 1978), *cert. den.*, 439 U.S. 1089 (1979); Feierstein v. The Gideons International, No. 84-418-B (D. Iowa 1985); Berger by Berger v. Rensselaer Central School Corporation, 982 F.2d 1160 (7th Cir.), *cert. den*, 508 U.S. 911 (1993) (school district policy allowing Gideons International to distribute their Bibles to fifth graders each year held to connote official endorsement of religious message and to be unconstitutional); Perumal v. Sadleback Valley Unified School District, 243 Cal.Rptr. 545, 198 C.A.3d 64 (Ct. App. 4th Dist.), *cert. den.*, 488 U.S. 93 (1988) (school board policy barring the distribution of literature from non-school groups held, as applied to the literature of a religious group, not to violate establishment clause); and Peck v. Upshur County Board of Education, 155 F.3d 274 (4th Cir. 1998) (school board policy allowing outside groups to set up tables on one day each year that made Bibles and other religious literature available, when board had historically allowed a number of nonreligious outside groups to distribute literature in its schools, held not to violate the establishment clause). *But see* Bacon v. Bradley-Bourbonnais High School District, 707 F.Supp. 1005 (C.D. Ill. 1989) (school district policy prohibiting the distribution of Gideon Bibles on the sidewalks in front of the public schools held to violate the free speech clause of the First Amendment).

[99] United States v. Board of Education for the School District of Philadelphia, 911 F.2d 882 (3d Cir. 1990) (state statute barring teachers from wearing religious attire held to serve compelling state interest in religious neutrality in the schools and not be be overridden by the requirement of Title VII of the Civil Rights Act of 1964 [42 U.S.C. 2000e *et seq.*] that employers make reasonable accommodation to the religious practices and beliefs of their employees); Cooper v. Eugene School District No. 4J, 301 Or. 358, 723 P.2d 298 (1986), *appeal dism'd for want of substantial federal question*, 480 U.S. 942 (1987) (suspension and revocation of teaching certificate of junior high school teacher who became a Sikh and persisted in wearing a white turban and white clothes in violation of state statute barring the wearing of any religious dress while engaged in the performance of duties as a teacher upheld). *See also* Mississippi Employment Security Commission V. McGlothin, 556 So.2d 324 (Miss. 1990), *cert. den.*, 498 U.S. 879 (1990) (teacher fired for insubordination because of her refusal to desist from wearing a religious head wrap held to be constitutionally entitled to unemployment benefits).

[100] *See* cases cited in n. 81.

[101] *See* cases cited in n. 86.

Thus, the courts have construed the establishment clause of the First Amendment to impose substantial constraints on government's involvement with religion in the public schools. Government is forbidden from

- sponsoring or promoting regular devotional exercises such as prayer and Bible reading;
- sponsoring prayers by a clergyman in graduation exercises;
- allowing students to elect volunteers to give invocations at athletic contests;
- using moments of silence as a way of promoting prayer;
- tailoring the curriculum to the precepts of any religious dogma;
- allowing outside parties to give religious instruction to students on the school premises during the school day;
- endorsing religion by means of wall plaques and paintings;
- allowing only the distribution of religious literature such as the Gideon Bible by outside parties;
- compelling students to take part in ceremonial or patriotic exercises involving professions of faith; and
- imposing curricular requirements that force students to violate their religious beliefs.

In addition, the First Amendment has been construed not to prohibit government from barring teachers from wearing religious attire.

ISSUES NOT YET DEFINITIVELY RESOLVED

Despite the plethora of judicial decisions concerning religion in the public schools, not all issues can be said as yet to have been definitively resolved. Two issues, in particular, stand out at the moment: (1) the constitutionality of student-initiated religious expression at high school commencement ceremonies, and (2) whether religious groups are constitutionally entitled to use school facilities outside of school hours for religious worship and instruction if the facilities are generally available for social, civic, and recreational purposes.

(a) Religious Expression at Secondary School Commencement Ceremonies

As noted above, the Supreme Court in *Lee v. Weisman, supra*, held the establishment clause to be violated by prayers given by a clergyman at the principal's invitation at a public secondary school's commencement exercise. The Court states that because of the "singular importance" of graduation to every student, the inclusion of prayers in the ceremony in effect coerced students into participating in "an explicit religious exercise" and was, therefore, unconstitutional.

Prior to *Weisman* the state and lower courts had been divided on the issue of the constitutionality of including invocations and benedictions in commencement ceremonies.[102] The Court's reasoning in *Weisman* appeared to some to be broad enough to lay the question to rest. But subsequently the United States Court of Appeals for the Fifth Circuit upheld as constitutional a school district policy permitting the graduating senior class to choose whether to have prayers at their graduation ceremonies and, if they decided to do so, to select student volunteers to give "nonsectarian, nonproselytizing invocations." In *Jones v. Clear Creek Independent School District*[103] the appellate court differentiated student-initiated and student-led prayers from the school-initiated and clergy-led prayers struck down in *Weisman*. The purpose and primary effect of the policy, the Fifth Circuit said, was "to solemnize graduation ceremonies," not to advance religion. It asserted that

---

[102] Compare Stein v. Plainwell Community Schools, 610 F.Supp. 43 (W.D. Mich.), aff'd in part, rev'd in part, 822 F.2d 1406 (6th Cir. 1987); Wood v. Mt. Lebanon Township School District, 342 F.Supp. 1293 (W.D. Pa. 1972); Grossberg v. Deusebio, 380 F.Supp. 285 (E.D. Va. 1974); Wiest v. Mt. Lebanon School District, 457 Pa. 166, 320 A.2d 363, *cert. den.*, 419 U.S. 967 (1974); Albright v. Board of Education of Granite School District, 765 F.Supp. 682 (D. Utah 1991), and Griffith v. Tehran, 794 F.Supp. 1054 (D. Kan. 1992), all upholding the inclusion of prayer as constitutional, *with* Graham v. Central Community School District of Decatur, 608 F.Supp. 531 (S.D. Iowa 1985); Kay v. David Douglas School District No. 40, 79 Or.App. 384, 719 P.2d 875 (1986), *vacated as moot*, 303 Or. 574, 738 P.2d 1389 (1987); Bennett v. Livermore Unified School District, 238 Cal.Rptr. 819, 193 C.A.3d 1012 (Ct.App. 1st Dist. 1987), Sands v. Morongo Unified School District, 281 Cal.Rptr. 34, 53 Cal.3d 862, 809 P.2d 809 (1991), *cert. den.*, 505 U.S. 1218 (1992), and Guidry v. Broussard, 897 F.2d 181 (5th Cir. 1990) (school's refusal to permit valedictorian to deliver speech with religious content at commencement ceremony upheld), all holding the inclusion of prayer in commencement ceremonies to be unconstitutional.

[103] 977 F.2d 963 (5th Cir. 1992), *cert. den.*, 508 U.S. 967 (1993).

the policy passively permitted prayer but did not endorse it; and it concluded that the policy had a less coercive effect on participation than the school's active involvement in *Weisman*, because any prayer at graduation that resulted emanated not from an authority figure from the school or clergy but from a student peer.

The Fifth Circuit has subsequently reaffirmed that ruling and it recently made clear in *Santa Fe Independent School District v. Doe*[104] that the nonsectarian and nonproselytizing nature of the student prayers is a constitutionally essential element.[105] However, two other federal courts of appeal have reached the opposite conclusion with respect to student elections to have, or not have, commencement prayer. In *Joint School District No. 241 v. Harris*[106] the Ninth Circuit, before the case was held to be mooted by the student's graduation, held such a policy to violate the establishment clause. It stated that the graduating class was as bound by the Constitution as the school district and that constitutional rights could not be subjected to majority vote. In *ACLU v. Blackhorse Pike Regional Board of Education*[107] the Third Circuit reached an identical conclusion, stating that a "student referendum does not erase the state's imprint from this graduation prayer."[108]

More recently, the U.S. Court of Appeals for the Eleventh Circuit upheld a variant of the *Clear Creek* policy. In *Adler v. Duval County School Board*[109] it found constitutional a policy permitting the graduating seniors to decide whether to have a brief opening and/or closing message at their graduation and, if they chose to do so, to select a student to give the message. The policy made no reference to prayer or an invocation and required that the student volunteer have total control over the content of the message and that it not be reviewed by school authorities. The court reasoned that the policy effectively divorced school officials from the decision whether to have a message as well as from its content and that, as a

---

[104] 168 F.3d 806 (1999).
[105] *See* Ingebretsen v. Jackson Public School District, 88 F.3d 274 (5th Cir. 1996), cert. den. sub nom. Moore v. Ingebretsen, 519 U.S. 968 (1996) and Santa Fe Independent School District v. Doe, 168 F.3d 806 (5th Cir. 1998), respectively.
[106] 41 F.3d 447 (9th Cir. 1994), *judgment vacated and case remanded with directions to dismiss as moot*, 515 U.S. 1154 (1996).
[107] 84 F.3d 1471 (3d Cir. 1996).
[108] *See also* Georon v. Loudoun County School Board, 844 F.Supp. 1097 (E.D. Va. 1993) (student-initiated and student-led prayer at commencement ceremony held unconstitutional).
[109] 206 F.3d 1070 (11th Cir.), *pet. for cert. filed*, 68 U.S.L.W. 3741 (2000).

Prayer and Religion in the Public Schools: What is, and is Not... 45

consequence, any religious content in the message could not be attributed to the state.

In another decision subsequently vacated as moot, the Ninth Circuit in *Doe v. Madison School District No. 321*[110] upheld a school district policy that permitted each high school administration to invite up to four students to speak at their school's commencement exercises. The students were chosen according to academic standing and could choose to deliver "an address, poem, reading, song, musical presentation, prayer, or any other pronouncement"; and the administration was barred from censoring or controlling any presentation. In upholding the policy, the court cited three factors: Students, not clergy, delivered the presentations; they were selected by a wholly neutral and secular criterion – academic standing; and they had complete autonomy over the content of their presentations.

The Supreme Court has not as yet decided to review a case specifically raising any of these variants in the context of graduation ceremonies. The Fifth Circuit decisions in *Clear Creek* and *Santa Fe* and the Ninth Circuit decision in *Harris* were appealed to the Court, but the Court chose not to review *Clear Creek* or this aspect of *Santa Fe*, and it vacated the *Harris* decision as moot. *Adler*, of course, is now pending on the Court's docket.

Nonetheless, substantial doubt now exists that the *Clear Creek* policy remains constitutional. In the part of *Santa Fe Independent School District v. Doe* that the Court did review, it struck down as unconstitutional a similar policy that applied to football games. As noted above (*see* p. 12), the Court held that notwithstanding the mechanism of student elections, the policy still violated all three of the tests the Court has employed for establishment clause cases – the *Lemon* test, the coercion test, and the endorsement test. It is, as a consequence, difficult to see how the same policy can pass constitutional muster simply because it involves a graduation ceremony.[111]

---

[110] 147 F.3d 832 (9th Cir.), *opinion withdrawn and decision vacated as moot*, 177 F.3d 789 (9th Cir. 1999).

[111] It might be noted that the result may not necessarily be the same at the public university level. In Tanford v. Brand, 104 F.3d 982 (7th Cir.), cert. den., 522 U.S. 814 (1997) the Seventh Circuit upheld as constitutional a public university's policy of inviting a religious leader to give an invocation and benediction to its graduation ceremony each year. The court differentiated this from Lee v. Weisman, *supra*, on the grounds the attendees were mature, attendance was wholly voluntary, peer pressure was minimal, and the prayers simply solemnized the event. Similarly, in Chaudhuri v. Tennessee, 130 F.3d 232 (6th Cir. 1997), cert. den., 523 U.S. 1024 (1998), the appellate court upheld a public university's practice of having a moment of silence as well as its

Nonetheless, additional litigation on this subject seems likely before it can be said to be fully settled.

(b) Use of School Facilities After School Hours for Religious Worship

As noted above (see p. 20), the Court in *Lamb's Chapel v. Center Moriches Free School District*[112] held that excluding religious groups from using school facilities for a film series offering a religious perspective, when the facilities are generally open for use by other social, civic, and recreational groups, violates the free speech clause of the First Amendment. Even in a nonpublic forum, it stated, restrictions on expression must be reasonable and viewpoint neutral. A public entity cannot open a public forum for the discussion of certain subjects, it asserted, and then bar particular viewpoints from being expressed. "The First Amendment," the Court stated, "forbids the government to regulate speech in ways that favor some viewpoints or ideas at the expense of others."[113]

Nonetheless, a number of subsequent decisions in the Second Circuit and one in the Fifth Circuit have held that even when a school district opens its facilities for general use by social, civic, and recreational groups and allows the discussion of secular subjects from a religious perspective, it is constitutionally permissible to bar the use of facilities for religious worship and instruction. Such discrimination, several courts have said, is permissible content or subject matter discrimination rather than impermissible viewpoint discrimination under the free speech clause.

The majority of the decisions have occurred in New York and involve a state statute permitting, but not requiring, local school districts to open school property for, *inter alia* social, civic and recreational meetings and entertainments, and other community welfare uses, "provided such uses are

---

previous practice of having nonsectarian prayers by local religious leaders and faculty members. The court said the latter practice served the legitimate secular purpose of solemnizing the occasion and would not be perceived by a reasonable observer as an attempt to "indoctrinate the audience." Any effect of endorsement, the court said, was "indirect, remote, and incidental." Similarly, it said, any entanglement with religion was *de minimis*.

[112] 508 U.S. 384 (1993).
[113] *Id.* at 394, quoting City Council of Los Angeles v. Taxpayers for Vincent, 466 U.S. 789, 804 (1984).

non-exclusive and open to the general public." The leading decision of *The Bronx Household of Faith v. Community School District No. 10*[114] challenged a New York City Board of Education regulation replicating that part of the state statute, but it also specifically barred outside groups from "conduct[ing] religious services or religious instruction on school premises after school." The regulation did permit outside groups to use school premises "for the purposes of discussing religious material or ... distributing such material."

A church that wanted to use a school gym for worship services for its growing congregation challenged the prohibition on free speech grounds. But the U.S. Court of Appeals for the Second Circuit upheld the regulation and stated that it "meticulously" complied with *Lamb's Chapel*. It allowed the discussion of secular subjects from a religious perspective, the court said, and simply excised in its entirety the category of religious worship and discussion. Such a subject matter limitation in a nonpublic forum, the appellate court held, was "reasonable and viewpoint neutral."

Similarly, in *The Good News Club v. Milford Central School*[115] the Second Circuit upheld a school district regulation that tracked the state statute and then barred the use of school premises "for religious purposes." Upon challenge by a Christian youth organization for children ages 6-12 that had been denied permission to meet in school facilities, the appellate court upheld its exclusion. The youth organization contended that other organizations such as the Boy Scouts were permitted to use school facilities to teach morals and values and that, as a consequence, the exclusion of a club because it taught morals and values from a Christian perspective constituted viewpoint discrimination. But the appellate court found that the Club was doing more than just offering a religious perspective on the secular subject of morality and, in fact, was engaging in religious worship and instruction. As a consequence, its exclusion, it said, was based on the content of its expression and not its viewpoint. Citing *Bronx Household* as authority, the court held the Club's exclusion to be constitutional.

Several other decisions in New York have similarly upheld regulations barring the use of school facilities for religious worship and instruction.[116]

---

[114] 127 F.3d 207 (2d Cir. 1998), *cert. den.*, 523 U.S. 934 (1998).
[115] 202 F.3d 502 (2d Cir.), *pet. for cert. filed*, 69 U.S.L.W. 3002 (2000).
[116] *See* Full Gospel Tabernacle v. community School District 27, 979 F.Supp.2d 214 (S.D. N.Y. 1997), *aff'd per curiam*, 164 F.3d 829 (2d Cir. 1999), *cert. den.*, 527 U.S. 1036 (1999); Saratoga Bible Training Institute, Inc. v. Schuylerville

Finally, in *Campbell v. St. Tammany's School Board*[117] the U.S. Court of Appeals for the Fifth Circuit upheld as constitutional a Louisiana school district regulation virtually identical to that in *Bronx Household of Faith*. Pursuant to the regulation, the school district had denied permission to a local chapter of the Christian Coalition to use school facilities for a prayer meeting. The Fifth Circuit said the regulation, by allowing the schools to be used for all but a few purposes, "skates close to establishing a designated public forum." But it concluded that "the restrictions are minimally sufficient to maintain the school buildings' status as a non-public forum." The court noted that "religion may be either a perspective on a topic such as marriage or ... a substantive activity in itself" and said that "in the latter case, the government's exclusion of the activity is discrimination based on content, not viewpoint." Agreeing with *Bronx Household*, the court concluded that religious services and instruction were "activities which may be excluded" consistent with the free speech clause.

Notwithstanding these decisions, such regulations seem likely to invite further litigation, and the Supreme Court may eventually have to resolve the matter.

CONCLUSION

Issues involving religion in the public schools can implicate a number of constitutional provisions but most particularly the establishment of religion, the free exercise of religion, and the freedom of speech clauses of the First Amendment. Because all of these clauses are worded as absolutes, it is sometimes ambiguous whether governmental involvement in a given situation is a permissible or required accommodation of religion or speech or a forbidden establishment of religion. But the essential meaning of this part of the First Amendment that has been elaborated by the courts over the last five decades appears to be that in the public schools government must be neutral regarding religious faith, serving neither as its agent or advocate nor as its adversary. Particularly in its role as educator, government is required to

---

Central School District, 18 F.Supp.2d 178 (N.D. N.Y. 1998); and Liberty Christian Center v. Watertown Board of Education, 8 F.Supp.2d 176 (1998).
[117] 206 F.3d 482 (5th Cir. 2000).

be objective and impartial about religion, not partisan. Government must maintain "strict neutrality, neither aiding nor opposing religion."[118]

Thus, government is not to be the agent of religious expression, nor is it to be its censor. As Justice O'Connor said in *Board of Education of Westside Community Schools v. Mergens*[119]:

> There is a crucial difference between government speech endorsing religion, which the Establishment Clause forbids, and private speech endorsing religion.

In other words, the free exercise and free speech clause of the Constitution have also been construed to provide substantial protection to private religious expression in the public schools.

Because matters concerning religion in the public schools touch deep emotions in the American public, controversies over the boundaries of religious expression in the public schools are certain to continue to arise. Indeed, as noted above, at least two issues currently remain unresolved and are likely to precipitate additional litigation. But unless and until the Supreme Court alters its basic interpretation of the First Amendment, the general principles of constitutional law in this area appear to be fairly well settled. As the Court has summarized:

> Government in our democracy, state and national, must be neutral in matters of religious theory, doctrine, and practice. It may not be hostile to any religion or to the advocacy of no-religion; and it may not aid, foster, or promote one religion or religious theory against another or even against the militant opposite. The First Amendment mandates governmental neutrality between religion and religion, and between religion and nonreligion.[120]

---

[118] Abington School District v. Schempp, *supra*, at 225.
[119] 496 U.S. 226, 250 (1990).
[120] Epperson v. Arkansas, *supra*, at 103-104.

BIBLIOGRAPHY

Alley, Robert S., 1932-
   School prayer: the Court, the Congress, and the First Amendment / Robert S. Alley.
   Published/Created: Buffalo, N.Y.: Prometheus Books, 1994.
   Description: 273 p.; 24 cm.
   ISBN: 0879758430 (cloth)
   Notes: Includes bibliographical references (p. 259-261) and index.
   Subjects: Prayer in the public schools--Law and legislation--United States.
   LC Classification: KF4162 .A94 1994
   Dewey Class No.: 344.73/0796 347.304796 20

Alley, Robert S., 1932-
   Without a prayer: religious expression in public schools / Robert S. Alley.
   Published/Created: Amherst, N.Y.: Prometheus Books, 1996.
   Description: 277 p.; 24 cm.
   ISBN: 1573920975 (alk. paper)
   Notes: Includes bibliographical references and index.
   Subjects: Prayer in the public schools--Law and legislation--United States.
   LC Classification: KF4162 .A944 1996
   Dewey Class No.: 344.73/0796 347.304796 20

America's constitutional heritage--prayer and our public schools.
   Published/Created: 1993.
   Related Author: Copyright Collection (Library of Congress)
   Description: 1 videocassette of 1: sd., col.; 1/2 in. viewing copy.
   Notes: Copyright: American Civil Liberties Union. DCR 1993; REG

27Dec93; PAu1-789-208.
Source used: copyright data base.
Source of Acquisition: Received: 3/24/94; viewing copy; copyright deposit--unpublished; Copyright Collection.
LC Classification: VAD 2868 (viewing copy)

Andryszewski, Tricia, 1956-
School prayer: a history of the debate / Tricia Andryszewski.
Published/Created: Springfield, NJ: Enslow Publishers, c1997.
Description: 104 p.; 23 cm.
ISBN: 0894909045
Notes: Includes bibliographical references (p. 96-102) and index.
Subjects: Prayer in the public schools--Law and legislation--United States--History.
Series: Issues in focus (Hillside, N.J.)
Variant Series: Issues in focus
LC Classification: KF4162.Z9 A54 1997
Dewey Class No.: 344.73/0796 21

Barton, David.
A guide to the school prayer & religious liberty debate / David Barton.
Published/Created: Aledo, TX: Rebuilder Press, c1995.
Description: 42 p.; 22 cm.
ISBN: 0925279498
Notes: Includes bibliographical references (p. 39-42).
Subjects: Prayer in the public schools--Law and legislation--United States. Freedom of religion--United States.
LC Classification: KF4162.Z9 B37 1995
Dewey Class No.: 344.73/0796 21

Barton, David.
America, to pray or not to pray?: a statistical look at what has happened since 39 million students were ordered to stop praying in public schools / by David Barton.
Published/Created: Aledo, Tex.: Specialty Research Associates, c1988.
Description: xiv, 196 p.: ill.; 22 cm.
Notes: Includes bibliographies.
Subjects: Prayer in the public schools--Government policy--United States. United States--Social conditions--1960-1980. United States--Social conditions--1980-
LC Classification: HN59 .B28 1988
Dewey Class No.: 306/.0973 19

Bedsole, Adolph. [from old catalog]
   The Supreme Court decision on Bible reading and prayer; America's black letter day.
   Published/Created: Grand Rapids, Baker Book House, 1964.
   Description: 55 p. 22 cm.
   Subjects: Religion in the public schools. [from old catalog]
   LC Classification: LC111 .B43

Black, Hugo LaFayette, 1886-1971.
   Papers of Hugo LaFayette Black, 1883-1976 (bulk 1926-1971)
   Description: 130,000 items. 513 containers plus 19 OV. 216 linear feet.
   Access Advisory: Restrictions apply.
   Biog./History Note: Associate justice of the U.S. Supreme Court, U.S. senator from Alabama, and lawyer.
   Summary: Family and general correspondence, memoranda, reports, notebooks, research materials, case files, legal and subject files, speeches and writings, printed and near-print materials, clippings, scrapbooks, and miscellany relating primarily to Black's service in the U.S. Senate (1927-1937) and on the Supreme Court (1937-1971). Topics include the New Deal, Nuremberg war crimes trials, politics in Alabama and elsewhere in the South, Tennessee Valley Authority and public utility regulation, public service employment, tariffs, Ku Klux Klan, public school racial integration, school prayer, and First Amendment freedoms (civil rights). Correspondents include Charles Austin Beard, Hollis Black, Josephine Foster Black, Harold H. Burton, Edmond Nathaniel Cahn, G. Harrold Carswell, Marquis William Childs, Jerome A. Cooper, David Jackson Davis, Irving Dilliard, Joseph Dorfman, Paul Howard Douglas, William O. Douglas, Clifford J. Durr, Virginia Foster Durr, John Paul Frank, Felix Frankfurter, Hugh Gladney Grant, Erwin N. Griswold, Clement F. Haynsworth, Lister Hill, Robert Houghwout Jackson, Peter Bryant Jarman, Nicholas Johnson, Arthur John Keeffe, Frida Laski, Harold Joseph Laski, Leonard Williams Levy, Charles Allan Madison. Louis F. Oberdorfer, Charles Alan Reich, Fred Rodell, Carl Sandburg, S. Sidney Ulmer, Earl Warren, Walter Francis White, Aubrey Willis Williams, and J. Skelly Wright.
   Notes: Dictaphone recordings, phonodiscs, magnetic tapes, and motion pictures transferred to the Library of Congress Motion Picture, Broadcasting and Recorded Sound Division. Photographs transferred to Library of Congress Prints and Photographs Division. MSS12831
   Finding Aids: Finding aid available in the Manuscript Reading Room.
   Source of Acquisition: Gift, Elizabeth (DeMeritte) Black and others, 1972-1998.
   Subjects: Beard, Charles Austin, 1874-1948 --Correspondence. Black, Hollis--Correspondence. Black, Josephine Foster, 1899-1951 --

Correspondence. Burton, Harold H. (Harold Hitz), 1888-1964 Correspondence. Cahn, Edmond Nathaniel, 1906-1964 -- Correspondence. Carswell, G. Harrold (George Harrold), 1919- Correspondence. Childs, Marquis William, 1903- --Correspondence. Cooper, Jerome A.--Correspondence. Davis, David Jackson, 1878-1938 --Correspondence. Dilliard, Irving, 1904- --Correspondence. Dorfman, Joseph, 1905- --Correspondence. Douglas, Paul Howard, 1892- -- Correspondence. Douglas, William O. (William Orville), 1898- Correspondence. Durr, Clifford J. (Clifford Judkins), 1899- Correspondence. Durr, Virginia Foster--Correspondence. Frank, John Paul, 1917- --Correspondence. Frankfurter, Felix, 1882-1965 -- Correspondence. Grant, Hugh Gladney, 1888-1972 --Correspondence. Griswold, Erwin N. (Erwin Nathaniel), 1904- Correspondence. Haynsworth, Clement F. (Clement Furman), 1912- Correspondence. Hill, Lister, 1894- --Correspondence. Jackson, Robert Houghwout, 1892-1954 --Correspondence. Jarman, Peterson Bryant, 1892-1955 -- Correspondence. Johnson, Nicholas, 1934- --Correspondence. Keeffe, Arthur John--Correspondence. Laski, Frida--Correspondence. Laski, Harold Joseph, 1893-1950 --Correspondence. Levy, Leonard Williams, 1923- --Correspondence. Madison, Charles Allan--Correspondence. Oberdorfer, Louis F. (Louis Falk), 1919- --Correspondence. Reich, Charles A.--Correspondence. Rodell, Fred, 1907- --Correspondence. Sandburg, Carl, 1878-1967 --Correspondence. Ulmer, S. Sidney-- Correspondence. Warren, Earl, 1891-1974 --Correspondence. White, Walter Francis, 1893-1955 --Correspondence. Williams, Aubrey Willis, 1890-1965 --Correspondence. Wright, J. Skelly--Correspondence. Ku Klux Klan (1915-) Tennessee Valley Authority. United States. Congress. Senate. United States. Constitution. United States. Supreme Court. Civil rights--United States. Constitutional amendments--United States. New Deal, 1933-1939. Nuremberg War Crime Trials, Nuremberg, Germany, 1946-1949. Public service employment--United States. Public utilities--United States. Religion in public schools. Segregation in education. School integration. Tariff--United States. Alabama--Politics and government. Southern States--Politics and government. United States--Economic policy--1933-1945. United States--Politics and government--1933-1945. Jurists. Lawyers. Senators, U.S. Congress--Alabama.

Block, Herbert, 1909- artist.
"What do they expect us to do - listen to the kids pray at home?" [graphic] / Herblock.
Published/Created: c1963.
Description: 1 drawing on layered paper: ink, graphite, and opaque white over graphite underdrawing; 57.3 x 38.4 cm. (sheet)

Use/Repro. Advisory: May be restricted: Information on reproduction rights available in LC P&P Restrictions Notebook.
Summary: Editorial cartoon showing a family seated at the dinner table eating, the father, with raging anger, holds a newspaper aloft, the headline reads "Supreme Court Ruling"; he demands of his cowering wife and obstinate children if he will now be obliged to "... listen to the kids pray at home?"
Notes: Published June 18, 1963 in the Washington Post. Copyright by Herblock, The Washington Post. Exhibited in: Herblock's History: Political Cartoons from the Crash to the Millennium, Library of Congress 2000-2001.
Subjects: Prayer in the public schools--1960-1970. Supreme Court decisions--1960-1970. Families--1960-1970. Eating & drinking--1960-1970. Anger--1960-1970.
Genre/Form: Editorial cartoons--1960-1970. Ink drawings--1960-1970.
LC Classification: Unprocessed [item]

Church of Scotland. General Assembly. Committee on Public Worship and Aids to Devotion.
Let us pray; a book of prayers for use in families, schools, and fellowships.
Published/Created: London, New York, Oxford University Press [1959]
Description: 95 p. 18 cm.
Subjects: Church of Scotland--Prayer-books and devotions--English.
LC Classification: BV245 .C45
Dewey Class No.: 264.13

Coniglio, John Vincent, 1963-
Rumors of angels / John Vincent Coniglio.
Published/Created: Eugene, Or.: Harvest House Publishers, c1994.
Description: 238 p.; 21 cm.
ISBN: 1565071719
Subjects: Prayer in the public schools--Law and legislation--United States--Fiction. Church and state--United States--Fiction.
Genre/Form: Christian fiction.
LC Classification: PS3553.O4885 R86 1994
Dewey Class No.: 813/.54 20

Cornish, Patty Jo.
An outrageous idea: natural prayer / Patty Jo Cornish; illustrations by James Hubbell.
Edition Information: 1st ed.
Published/Created: San Diego, Calif.: Hilltop House Publishers, c1996.
Description: 108 p.: ill.; 21 cm.

ISBN: 0961371714
Subjects: Prayer. Spiritual life. Prayer in the public schools.
LC Classification: BL560 .C66 1996
Dewey Class No.: 291.4/3 20

Daum, Annette.
Assault on the Bill of Rights: the Jewish stake: religious test for office, scientific creationism, censorship in the schools, prayer in the public schools, religious celebrations in the schools, missionary activities, aid to parochial schools, abortion rights / Annette Daum.
Published/Created: New York, N.Y. (838 Fifth Ave., New York 10021): Published by the Union of American Hebrew Congregations for the Commission on Social Action of Reform Judaism, [1982?]
Description: ii, 145 p.: ill.; 28 cm.
Notes: Cover title. Bibliography: p. 136.
Subjects: Religion and state--United States. Civil rights--United States. Freedom of religion--United States. Judaism and state--United States.
LC Classification: BL2525 .D38 1982
Dewey Class No.: 323.44/2/0973 19

Dolbeare, Kenneth M.
The school prayer decisions from court policy to local practice [by] Kenneth M. Dolbeare and Phillip E. Hammond.
Published/Created: Chicago, University of Chicago Press [1971]
Related Author: Hammond, Phillip E., joint author.
Description: xi, 164 p. 23 cm.
ISBN: 0226155153
Subjects: Religion in the public schools--Law and legislation United States.
LC Classification: KF4162 .D64
Dewey Class No.: 344/.73/0796

Donovan, Teresa L.
Voluntary school prayer: judicial dilemma, proposed solutions / by Teresa L. Donovan, Marcella C. Donovan, and Joseph J. Piccione.
Published/Created: [Washington, D.C.] (721 Second St., N.E., Washington 20002): Child and Family Protection Institute of the Free Congress Research & Education Foundation, [c1984]
Related Author: Donovan, Marcella C. Piccione, Joseph.
Description: x, 83 p.; 22 cm.
Notes: Includes bibliographies.
Subjects: Prayer in the public schools--Law and legislation--United States.
Series: Currents in family policy

LC Classification: KF4162.Z9 D66 1984
Dewey Class No.: 344.73/0796 347.304796 19

Dudley, Mark E.
Engel v. Vitale (1962): religion in the schools / by Mark E. Dudley.
Edition Information: 1st ed.
Published/Created: New York: Twenty-First Century Books, c1995.
Description: vii, 96 p.: ill.; 24 cm.
ISBN: 0805039163 (acid-free paper)
Summary: Points out that although a 1962 Supreme Court case decided that official prayers in public schools are unconstitutional, the issue of separation of church and state remains.
Notes: Includes bibliographical references (p. 87-94) and index.
Subjects: Engel, Steven I.--Trials, litigation, etc.--Juvenile literature. Vitale, William J.--Trials, litigation, etc.--Juvenile literature. Engel, Steven I.--Trials, litigation, etc. Vitale, William J.--Trials, litigation, etc. Prayer in the public schools--Law and legislation--United States--Juvenile literature. Religion in the public schools--Law and legislation United States--Juvenile literature. Church and state--United States--Juvenile literature. Religion in the public schools. Church and state.
Series: Supreme Court decisions (New York, N.Y.)
Variant Series: Supreme Court decisions
LC Classification: KF228.E54 D83 1995
Dewey Class No.: 344.73/0796/0269 347.3047960269 20

Duke, David W.
Principles of liberty: a practical guide to constitutional law / [David W. Duke].
Published/Created: Fullerton, CA: R.C. Law & Co., c1991.
Description: ii, 170 p.; 22 cm.
ISBN: 0939925656
Notes: Includes index.
Subjects: Civil rights--United States--Popular works. Prayer in the public schools--Law and legislation--United States--Popular works. Abortion--Law and legislation--United States--Popular works. Obscenity (Law)--United States--Popular works.
LC Classification: KF4750 .D85 1991
Dewey Class No.: 342.73/085 347.30285 20

Durham, James R., 1938-
Secular darkness: religious right involvement in Texas public education, 1963-1989 / James R. Durham.
Published/Created: New York: P. Lang, c1995.
Description: xi, 124 p.; 24 cm.

ISBN: 0820425435 (alk. paper)
Notes: Includes bibliographical references (p. [113]-124).
Subjects: Church and education--Texas. Religion in the public schools--Texas. Prayer in the public schools--Texas. Fundamentalism.
Series: American university studies. Series IX, History, 0740-0462; v. 167
LC Classification: LC111 .D87 1995
Dewey Class No.: 377/.1/09764 20

Dusek, Clare Lynn.
Prayer, piety and the Supreme Court [microform]: a case study of the Supreme Court decision concerning state-sponsored prayer in public schools / by Clare Lynn Dusek.
Published/Created: 1973.
Description: x, 134 leaves.
Notes: Thesis (M.A.)--University of Houston. Microfilm. Ann Arbor, Mich.: University Microfilms International, 1973. 1 microfilm reel; 35 mm.
LC Classification: Microfilm 51114 (E)

Emancipating school prayer / edited with an introduction by Harry V. Jaffa.
Published/Created: Claremont, Calif.: Claremont Institute, c1996.
Related Author: Jaffa, Harry V. Salvatori Center for the American Constitution.
Description: x, 46 p.; 22 cm.
ISBN: 0930783263
Notes: "The Salvatori Center for the American Constitution"--Cover.
Subjects: Prayer in the public schools--Law and legislation—United States--States--Popular works. Prayer in the public schools--Law and legislation—United States--Popular works.
LC Classification: KF4162.Z9 E+

Fenwick, Lynda Beck, 1944-
Should the children pray?: a historical, judicial, and political examination of public school prayer / Lynda Beck Fenwick.
Published/Created: Waco, Tex.: Markham Press Fund of Baylor University Press, c1989.
Description: 249 p.; 24 cm.
ISBN: 0918954517 (alk. paper) :
Notes: Includes bibliographical references (p. 237-242) and index.
Subjects: Prayer in the public schools--United States--History. Freedom of religion--United States--History. Church and state--United States--History.
LC Classification: LC111 .F44 1989

Dewey Class No.: 377/.14 20

Gay, Kathlyn.
    Church and state: government and religion in the United States / Kathlyn Gay.
    Published/Created: Brookfield, Conn.: Millbrook Press, c1992.
    Description: 128 p.: ill.; 24 cm.
    ISBN: 1562940635 (lib. bdg.)
    Summary: Discusses the division between government and religion in the United States and problems in such areas as school prayer, public displays of religious symbols, and religious practices that violate the law.
    Notes: Includes bibliographical references (p. 122-123) and index.
    Subjects: Church and state--United States--Juvenile literature. Religion in the public schools--United States--Juvenile literature. Religion and politics--United States--Juvenile literature. Freedom of religion--United States--Juvenile literature. Church and state. Freedom of religion.
    Series: Issue and debate
    LC Classification: BR516 .G37 1992
    Dewey Class No.: 322/.1/0973 20

Haas, Carol.
    Engel v. Vitale: separation of church and state / Carol Haas.
    Published/Created: Hillside, NJ, U.S.A.: Enslow Publishers, c1994.
    Description: 128 p.: ill.; 24 cm.
    ISBN: 0894904612 (library ed.)
    Notes: Includes bibliographical references (p. 125-126) and index.
    Subjects: Engel, Steven I.--Trials, litigation, etc.--Juvenile literature. Vitale, William J.--Trials, litigation, etc.--Juvernile literature. Engel, Steven I.--Trials, litigation, etc. Vitale, William J.--Trials, litigation, etc. Prayer in the public schools--Law and legislation--United States--Juvenile literature. Religion in the public schools--Law and legislation United States--Juvenile literature. Church and state--United States--Juvenile literature. Religion in the public schools. Church and state.
    Series: Landmark Supreme Court cases
    LC Classification: KF228.E54 H33 1994
    Dewey Class No.: 344.73/0796 347.304796 20

Jones, Aubrey, 1941-
    A moment of silence / Aubrey Jones.
    Published/Created: Nashville: T. Nelson, c1995.
    Description: 214 p.; 21 cm.
    ISBN: 0785279709
    Notes: "A Jan Dennis book."

Subjects: High school teachers--Fiction. Prayer in the public schools--Fiction.
Genre/Form: Christian fiction.
LC Classification: PS3560.O4575 M66 1995
Dewey Class No.: 813/.54 20

Keynes, Edward.
The Court vs. Congress: prayer, busing, and abortion / Edward Keynes with Randall K. Miller.
Published/Created: Durham: Duke University Press, 1989.
Related Miller, Randall K.
Description: xx, 400 p.; 25 cm.
ISBN: 0822309513 (alk. paper) 0822309688 (pbk.: alk. paper)
Notes: Includes index. Bibliography: p. [313]-380.
Subjects: United States. Supreme Court. Judicial review--United States. Legislative power--United States. Prayer in the public schools--Law and legislation--United States. Busing for school integration--Law and legislation--United States. Abortion--Law and legislation--United States.
LC Classification: KF4575 .K49 1989
Dewey Class No.: 347.73 347.307 20

Kik, Jacob Marcellus, 1903-
The Supreme Court and prayer in the public school.
Published/Created: Philadelphia, Presbyterian and Reformed Pub. Co., 1963.
Description: 40 p. 23cm.
Subjects: Prayer in the public schools--Law and legislation--United States.
Series: International library of philosophy and theology: Biblical and theological studies series
Variant Series: International library of philosophy and theology: Biblical and theological studies
LC Classification: KF4162.Z9 K5

Laubach, John Herbert.
School prayers; Congress, the courts, and the public.
Published/Created: Washington, Public Affairs Press [1969]
Description: ix, 178 p. 24 cm.
Notes: Includes bibliographical references.
Subjects: Prayer in the public schools--Law and legislation--United States.
LC Classification: KF4162 .L3
Dewey Class No.: 340

Law and religion: a critical anthology / edited by Stephen M. Feldman.
  Published/Created: New York: New York University Press, c2000.
  Related Author: Feldman, Stephen M., 1955-
  Description: xi, 483 p.; 26 cm.
  ISBN: 0814726798 (paper: acid-free paper) 081472678X (cloth: acid-free paper)
  Contents: Religious freedom in America: three stories / Steven D.Smith -- The widening gyres of religion and law / Martin E. Marty -- A new discourse and practice / Winnifred Fallers Sullivan -- The Rev. John Witherspoon and the Constitutional Convention / Marci A. Hamilton -- The place of religious argument in a free and democratic society / Robert Audi -- A new order of religious freedom / Richard John Neuhaus -- The other side of religion / William P. Marshall -- Liberal democracy and religious morality / Michael J. Perry -- The Pope's submarine / John H. Garvey -- Why the state must subordinate religion / Scott C. Idleman -- Equal regard / Christopher Eisgruber and Lawrence Sager -- The incommensurability of religion / Abner S. Greene -- Questioning the value of accommodating religion / Mark V. Tushnet -- A christian America and the separation of church and state / Stephen M. Feldman -- Jewish voices and religious freedom: a Jewish critique of critical Jewish thinking / Mark A. Graber -- A crack in the wall: pluralism, prayer and pain in the public schools / Frank S. Ravitch -- Secular fundamentalism, religious fundamentalism, and the search for truth in contemporary America / Daniel O. Conkle -- The constitutional tradition: a perplexing legacy / Ronald F. Thiemann -- Toward a normative framework of a love-based C19. Toward a normative framework of a love-based community / Anthony E. Cook -- Mission impossible: settling the just bounds between church and state / Stanley Fish -- Liberal thought and religion in custody and visitation cases / Linda Lacey -- There can be only one: law, religion, grammar and social organization in the United States / Larry Cat Backer.
  Notes: Includes bibliographical references and index.
  Subjects: Church and state--United States. Law and religion--United States. Law and religion.
  Series: Critical America
  LC Classification: KF4865 .L39 2000
  Dewey Class No.: 342.73/0852 21

Loren, Julia C.
  Engel v. Vitale: prayer in the public schools / by Julia C. Loren.
  Published/Created: San Diego, CA: Lucent Books, c2001.
  Description: 96 p.: ill.; 24 cm.
  ISBN: 1560067322 (alk. paper)
  Summary: Points out that although a 1962 Supreme Court case decided

that official prayers in public schools are unconstitutional, the issue of separation of church and state remains.
Notes: Includes bibliographical references (p. 87-90) and index.
Subjects: Engel, Steven I.--Trials, litigation, etc.--Juvenile literature. Vitale, William J.--Trials, litigation, etc.--Juvenile literature. Engel, Steven I.--Trials, litigation, etc. Vitale, William J.--Trials, litigation, etc. Prayer in the public schools--Law and legislation--United States--Juvenile literature. Religion in the public schools--Law and legislation United States--Juvenile literature. Church and state--United States--Juvenile literature. Religion in the public schools. Church and state. Trials.
Series: Famous trials
LC Classification: KF228.E54 L67 2001
Dewey Class No.: 344.73/0796 21

Menendez, Albert J.
School prayer and other religious issues in American public education: a bibliography / Albert J. Menendez.
Published/Created: New York: Garland, 1985.
Description: x, 168 p.; 23 cm.
ISBN: 0824087755 (alk. paper)
Notes: Includes indexes.
Subjects: Prayer in the public schools--United States--Bibliography. Religion in the public schools--United States Bibliography. Religious education--United States--Bibliography. Prayer in the public schools--Law and legislation--United States--Bibliography.
Series: Garland reference library of social science; v. 291.
Variant Series: Garland reference library of social science; vol. 291
LC Classification: Z5815.U5 M46 1985 LC405
Dewey Class No.: 016.377/1 19

Muir, William Ker.
Prayer in the public schools; law and attitude change [by] William K. Muir, Jr.
Published/Created: Chicago, University of Chicago Press [1967]
Description: ix, 170 p. 21 cm.
Notes: Bibliographical footnotes.
Subjects: Prayer in the public schools--Law and legislation--United States. Prayer in the public schools--United States.
LC Classification: KF4162 .M8
Dewey Class No.: 344/.73/0796

Murray, William J. (William Joseph), 1946-
Let us pray: a plea for prayer in our schools / William J. Murray.

Edition Information: 1st ed.
Published/Created: New York: W. Morrow, c1995.
Description: xvii, 205 p.; 22 cm.
ISBN: 0688145639 (acid-free paper) :
Notes: Includes bibliographical references (p. 203-205).
Subjects: Prayer in the public schools--Law and legislation--United States.
LC Classification: KF4162 .M87 1995
Dewey Class No.: 344.73/0796 347.304796 20

Neamon, Anne.
Defending the First Amendment [sound recording]: church/state Christian morality explained, the Nativity scene, a part of Christmas, the United States Supreme Court / Anne Neamon.
Published/Created: [United States]: A. Neamon, 1995.
Related Author: Citizens for God & Country (U.S.)
Description: 1 sound cassette (37 min.): analog.
Summary: Presents an interview with Anne Neamon, the national coordinator of Citizens for God & Country, concerning her successful Supreme Court case regarding the separation of church and state and the First Amendment to the Constitution. The ruling by the court permits a Nativity scene to be displayed on government property during the Christmas season in Washington, D.C. Includes discussion and commentary on the inclusion of daily prayer in public schools.
Subjects: Neamon, Ann--Interviews. United States. Constitution. 1st Amendment. United States. Supreme Court. Church and state--Washington (D.C.) Crèches (Nativity scenes)--Washington (D.C.) Government property--Washington (D.C.) Freedom of religion--Washington (D.C.) Prayer in the public schools--United States.
LC Classification: RYG 8269

Neamon, Anne.
God & country vs. atheism: exploitations of U.S. Supreme Court decision on school prayers in threat to national security / Anne Neamon.
Edition Information: 4th ed.
Published/Created: McLean, Va.: Citizens for God & Country, 1977, c1976.
Description: ix, 50, 39, [19] p.: ill.; 28 cm.
Subjects: Prayer in the public schools--Law and legislation--United States.
LC Classification: KF4162 .N4 1977
Dewey Class No.: 344.73/0796 347.304796 19

Neamon, Anne.
　God and country vs atheism: exploitations of U.S. Supreme Court decisions on school prayer in threat to national security / Anne Neamon.
　Edition Information: 2d ed.
　Published/Created: Washington: National Back to God Movement], 1976.
　Related National Back to God Movement.
　Description: vii, 37, 37 p.: ill.; 29 cm.
　Notes: Cover title.
　Subjects: Religion in the public schools--Law and legislation United States.
　LC Classification: KF4162.Z9 N4 1976
　Dewey Class No.: 344/.73/0793

Neuser, Wolfgang.
　Schulgottesdienst als sabbatliche Unterbrechung des Schulalltags, eine Chance für Schule und Kirche / vorgelegt von Wolfgang Neuser.
　Published/Created: Siegen: [s.n.], 1992 (Darmstadt: Dissertations Druck)
　Description: 463 p.; 21 cm.
　Notes: Spine Schulgottesdienst, Chance für Schule und Kirche. Thesis (doctoral)--Universität-Gesamthochschule Siegen, 1992. Includes bibliographical references (p. 449-463).
　Subjects: Prayer in the public schools--Germany. Religion in the public schools--Germany.
　LC Classification: LC116.G3 N48 1992

Neutral against God [sound recording]: school prayer and the First Amendment.
　Published/Created: Los Angeles, Calif.: Pacifica Radio Archive, p1983.
　Related Author: Amos, Deborah. Bill of Rights Radio Education Project. Pacifica Radio Archive.
　Description: 1 sound cassette (29 min.): analog.
　Publisher Number: PZ0047.04 Pacifica Radio Archive
　Summary: In this 1982 radio broadcast, host Deborah Amos explores the controversy surrounding school prayer, focusing on the First Amendment's principle of church-state separation. Includes interviews, speeches, and journalistic analysis.
　Notes: Presented by the Bill of Rights Radio Education Project. Issued also on reel.
　Subjects: Prayer in the public schools--Law and legislation--United States.
　LC Classification: KF4162 RYA 3924

New Jersey. Legislature. Senate. Judiciary Committee.
   Public hearing before Senate Judiciary Committee on moment of
   silence: held December 22, 1982, Room 114, State House Annex,
   Trenton, New Jersey.
   Published/Created: Trenton, N.J.: The Committee, [1982]
   Description: 24 p., [1] leaf of plates: ill.; 28 cm.
   Notes: Cover title.
   Subjects: New Jersey. Office of the Attorney General. Prayer in the
   public schools--Law and legislation--New Jersey.
   LC Classification: KFN1811.3 .J8 1982b
   Dewey Class No.: 377/.1 19

New York (State). Legislature. Assembly. Committee on Colleges,
   Academies and Common Schools.
   Barnard's report on the use of the Bible in common schools.
   Published/Created: Providence: Knowles, Vose & Co., 1838.
   Related Author: Barnard, Daniel D. (Daniel Dewey), 1797-1861.
   Miscellaneous Pamphlet Collection (Library of Congress)
   Description: 16 p.; 19 cm.
   References: Checklist Amer. imprints 51941
   Subjects: Prayer in the public schools--New York (State)
   LC Classification: AC901 .M5 vol. 355, no. 11

O'Hair, Madalyn Murray.
   An atheist epic: the complete unexpurgated story of how Bible and
   prayers were removed from the public schools of the United States /
   Madalyn O'Hair.
   Edition Information: 2nd ed.
   Published/Created: Austin, Tex.: American Atheist Press, 1989.
   Description: xii, 302 p.: ill., ports.; 21 cm.
   ISBN: 0910309892 :
   Subjects: O'Hair, Madalyn Murray. Prayer in the public schools--United
   States--History. Atheists--United States--Biography.
   LC Classification: LC111 .O48 1989
   Dewey Class No.: 377/.14 20

Prayer and religion in public schools
   Published/Created: Huntington, N.Y.: Nova Science, 2002.
   Projected Pub. Date: 0201
   Description: p. cm.
   ISBN: 1590331435
   LC Control Number: 2001058736

Prayer in public schools and the Constitution, 1961-1992 / edited with an introduction by Robert Sikorski.
Published/Created: New York: Garland Pub., 1993.
Related Author: Sikorski, Robert, 1949-
Description: 3 v.; 24 cm.
ISBN: 0815312725 (v. 1: alk. paper)
Contents: v. 1. Government-sponsored religious activities in public schools and the Constitution.-- v. 2. Moments of silence in public schools and the Constitution. -- v. 3. Protecting religious speech in public schools. The Establishment and free exercise clauses in the public arena.
Notes: Includes bibliographical references.
Subjects: Prayer in the public schools--Law and legislation--United States.
Series: Controversies in constitutional law
LC Classification: KF4162 .P73 1993
Dewey Class No.: 344.73/0796 347.304796 20

Randolph, J. W. [from old catalog]
The everlasting joy. Adapted to the use of public and private worship, Sabbath Schools, prayer meetings, also, anniversary occasions, etc., etc., by J. W. Randolph.
Published/Created: Galveston, Texas, Thos. Goggan & Bro. c1864.
Description: 83 p. cm.
Notes: Hymn collection.
LC Classification: M2198.R21 R8

Ravitch, Frank S., 1966-
School prayer and discrimination: the civil rights of religious minorities and dissenters / Frank S. Ravitch.
Published/Created: Boston: Northeastern University Press, 1999.
Description: xiii, 273 p.; 24 cm.
ISBN: 1555533922 (cloth: acid-free paper)
Notes: Includes bibliographical references (p. 213-263) and index.
Subjects: Prayer in the public schools--Law and legislation--United States. Religious minorities--Legal status, laws, etc.--United States. Freedom of religion--United States.
LC Classification: KF4162 .R38 1999
Dewey Class No.: 344.73/09796 21

Religion and the schools: from prayer to public aid.
Published/Created: [Washington] National School Public Relations Association [1970]
Related Author: National School Public Relations Association.

Description: 55 p. 28 cm.
Notes: Cover title. "Produced by the staff of Education U.S.A."
Bibliography: p. 52-54.
Subjects: Religion in the public schools--United States.
Series: Education USA special report.
Variant Series: Education U.S.A. special report
LC Classification: LC111 .R44
Dewey Class No.: 377/.0973

Rice, Charles E.
The Supreme Court and public prayer, the need for restraint.
Published/Created: New York, Fordham University Press [1964]
Description: xiii, 202 p. 24 cm.
Notes: Includes bibliographical references.
Subjects: Religion in the public schools--Law and legislation United States.
LC Classification: KF4162 .R5
Dewey Class No.: 377.102673

School prayer constitutional amendment: report of the Committee on the Judiciary, United States Senate, on S.J. Res. 212 together with minority and additional views.
Published/Created: Washington: U.S. G.P.O., 1984.
Related Author: United States. Congress. Senate. Committee on the Judiciary.
Description: iii, 82 p.; 24 cm.
Notes: Distributed to some depository libraries in microfiche. "January 24 ... 1984." Item 1008-C, 1008-D (microfiche) Includes bibliographical references.
Subjects: Prayer in the public schools--Law and legislation--United States.
Series: United States. Congress. Senate. Report; no. 98-347.
Variant Series: Report / 98th Congress, 2d session, Senate; no. 98-347
LC Classification: KF31 .J8 1984
Dewey Class No.: 344.73/0796 347.304796 19
Govt. Doc. No.: Y 1.1/5:98-347

Schwengel, Fred, 1907-
School prayer amendment debate. Sound recording [by] Rep. Schwengel [and] Rep. Wylie.
Published/Created: [New York] Encyclopedia Americana/CBS News Audio Resource Library 1971.
Related Author: Wylie, Chalmers, joint author. Jackson, Henry M. (Henry Martin), 1912-1983.

Description: 1 cassette. 2-track. mono.
Publisher Number: 11712
Contents: Side A. Schwengel, F. & Wylie, C. School prayer amendment debate. Jackson, H. W. Declaration of candidacy, pt. 1.-Side B. Jackson, H. M. Declaration of candidacy, pt. 2.
Notes: With study guides. Preservation master. Washington, D.C.: Library of Congress Magnetic Recording Laboratory, 1978. On 1 sound tape reel: analog, 7 1/2 ips, double track, mono.; 10 in. 262 conversion. 305 conversion.
Subjects: Religion in the public schools--Law and legislation United States. Presidents--United States--Election--1972.
Series: Vital history cassettes. Nov., 1971, no. 2.
Variant Series: Vital history cassettes, Nov., 1971; no. 2
LC Classification: RZA 0755 LWO 12184 R16 B1 (preservation master)

Schwengel, Fred. [from old catalog]
School prayer amendment debate. [Sound recording] [By] Rep. Schwengel [and] Rep. Wylie.
Published/Created: [n.p.] Encyclopedia Americana/CBS News Audio Resource Library 11712. [1972]
Wylie, Chalmers, [from old catalog] joint author.
Description: p. 1 cassette. 2 1/2 x 4 in.
Notes: Vital history cassettes, no. 2, Nov. '71. Distributed by Grolier Educational Corp., New York. Recorded Nov. 8, 1971 in Washington, D.C. Duration: 10 min., 54 sec. SUMMARY: The two Congressmen, interviewed together by CBS News, debate the proposed amendment to the Constitution which would allow prayers to be read in public schools.
With: Jackson, H. W. Declaration of candidacy.
Subjects: Religion in the public schools--Law and legislation United States. [from old catalog]
Series: Vital history cassettes, no. 2, N v. '71. [from old catalog]
LC Classification: D411

Shedd, William Greenough Thayer, 1820-1894.
Motives to prayer for colleges: an address delivered in the First Presbyterian Church in the City of New York, February 26, 1863 / by William G.T. Shedd.
Published/Created: [New York: s.n., 1863]
Related Author: YA Pamphlet Collection (Library of Congress)
Description: 16 p.; 23 cm.
Subjects: Prayer in the public schools.
LC Classification: YA 11518

Smith, Rodney K.
  Public prayer and the Constitution: a case study in constitutional interpretation / by Rodney K. Smith.
  Published/Created: Wilmington, Del.: Scholarly Resources, 1987.
  Description: xv, 305 p.; 24 cm.
  ISBN: 0842022600 :
  Notes: Includes bibliographical references and index.
  Subjects: Prayer in the public schools--Law and legislation--United States.
  LC Classification: KF4162 .S63 1987
  Dewey Class No.: 344.73/0796 347.304796 19

Sorensen, Susan.
  Kit Cat and the whirling watches: the story of a nation built by prayer / Susan Sorensen and Joette Whims.
  Published/Created: San Juan Capistrano, CA: Joy Pub., c1994.
  Projected Pub. Date: 9401
  Related Author: Whims, Joette.
  Description: p. cm.
  ISBN: 0939513331 :
  Notes: Includes bibliographical references and index.
  Subjects: National Day of Prayer. Prayer--United States--History. Children's stories, American. Religion in the public schools--United States--Law and legislation. United States--Religious life and customs.
  LC Classification: BL2525 .S583 1994
  Dewey Class No.: 291.4/3/0973 20

Stamp, Robert M.
  Religious exercises in elementary and secondary schools / Robert M. Stamp.
  Published/Created: [Toronto], Ont.: Ministry of Education: Ontario Institute for Studies in Education [distributor], c1986.
  Related Author: Ontario. Ministry of Education.
  Description: v, 39 p.; 30 cm.
  ISBN: 0772915474 (pbk.)
  Notes: Bibliography: p. 37-38.
  Subjects: Prayer in the public schools--Ontario. Prayer in the public schools--Canada.
  LC Classification: LC114.2.O6 S73 1986

Storm over the Supreme Court. Part 2: The school prayer case [Motion picture]
  Published/Created: [n.p.] CBS News, 1963.
  Related Author: Columbia Broadcasting System, inc. CBS News. [from

old catalog]
Description: p. 54 min. sd. b&w. 16 mm.
Notes: Telecase on the CBS-TV documentary show CBS reports.
CREDITS: Producer, William Peters; reporter Eric Sevareid.
SUMMARY: Follows events which produced the Supreme Court decision against prayer in schools in the case of Engel vs. Vitale. Analyses the controversy over the decision.
Subjects: Religion in the public schools--Law and legislation United States. [from old catalog]

The Supreme Court and the '84 election [sound recording].
Published/Created: Washington, D.C.: National Public Radio, p1984.
Related Author: Totenberg, Nina. National Public Radio (U.S.)
Description: 1 sound cassette (17 min.): analog.
Publisher Number: AT-841002 National Public Radio
Summary: Examines the history of past Supreme Court appointments, then focuses on those trends in American law and human rights, including discrimination, citizen access to courts, prayer in schools, abortion, and government regulation of business, that would be ripe for reversal should President Reagan name two or more justices to the court.
Notes: Originally broadcast Oct. 2, 1984, on the National Public Radio program entitled All things considered.
Cast: Reporter, Nina Totenberg.
Subjects: Reagan, Ronald. United States. Supreme Court--Officials and employees Selection and appointment. Judges--Selection and appointment--United States. Civil rights--United States.
LC Classification: KF8742 RYA 7617

United States. Congress. House. Committee on the Judiciary. Subcommittee on Courts, Civil Liberties, and the Administration of Justice.
Prayer in public schools and buildings--federal court jurisdiction: hearings before the Subcommittee on Courts, Civil Liberties, and the Administration of Justice of the Committee on the Judiciary, House of Representatives, Ninety-sixth Congress, second session, on S. 450 ... July 29, 30, August 19, 21, and September 9, 1980.
Published/Created: Washington: U.S. G.P.O., 1981.
Description: iv, 976 p.; 24 cm.
Notes: "Serial no. 63." Item 1020 Includes bibliographies.
Subjects: United States. Supreme Court. Jurisdiction--United States. Prayer in the public schools--Law and legislation--United States.
LC Classification: KF27 .J857 1980a
Dewey Class No.: 344.73/0796 347.304796 19

United States. Congress. House. Committee on the Judiciary. Subcommittee on the Constitution.
Religious freedom protection: hearing before the Subcommittee on the Constitution of the Committee on the Judiciary, House of Representatives, One Hundred Fourth Congress, second session, on H.J. Res. 184 ... July 23, 1996.
Published/Created: Washington: U.S. G.P.O.: For sale by the U.S. G.P.O., Supt. of Docs., Congressional Sales Office, 1997.
Description: iv, 399 p.; 24 cm.
ISBN: 0160554454
Notes: Distributed to some depository libraries in microfiche. Shipping list no.: 97-0372-P. "Serial no. 123." Includes bibliographical references.
Subjects: Freedom of religion--United States. Religion in the public schools--Law and legislation United States. Prayer in the public schools--Law and legislation--United States. Constitutional amendments--United States.
LC Classification: KF27 .J8565 1996j
Dewey Class No.: 342.73/0852 21

United States. Congress. Senate. Committee on the Judiciary. Subcommittee on Constitutional Amendments.
School prayer. Hearings, Eighty-ninth Congress, second session.
Published/Created: Washington, U.S. Govt. Print. Off., 1966.
Description: vi, 884 p. illus., maps (1 fold.) 24 cm.
Notes: Hearings held Aug. 1-8, 1966. "Senate joint resolution 148, relating to prayer in public schools."
Subjects: Prayer in the public schools--Law and legislation--United States.
LC Classification: KF26 .J836 1966
Dewey Class No.: 340

United States. Congress. Senate. Committee on the Judiciary. Subcommittee on the Constitution.
Constitutional amendment relating to school prayer: hearing before the Subcommittee on the Constitution of the Committee on the Judiciary, United States Senate, Ninety-ninth Congress, first session, on S.J. Res. 2 ... June 19, 1985.
Published/Created: Washington: U.S. G.P.O., 1986.
Description: iv, 264 p.: ill.; 24 cm.
Notes: Distributed to some depository libraries in microfiche. Shipping list no.: 86-184-P. "Serial no. J-99-33." Item 1042-A, 1042-B (microfiche) Bibliography: p. 71-79.
Subjects: Prayer in the public schools--Law and legislation--United

States.
Series: United States. Congress. Senate. S. hrg.; 99-386.
Variant Series: S. hrg.; 99-386
LC Classification: KF26 .J8359 1985b
Dewey Class No.: 344.73/0796 347.304796 19

United States. Congress. Senate. Committee on the Judiciary. Subcommittee on the Constitution.
Voluntary school prayer constitutional amendment: hearings before the Subcommittee on the Constitution of the Committee on the Judiciary, United States Senate, Ninety-eighth Congress, first session, on S.J. Res. 73 ... and S.J. Res. 212 ... April 29, May 2, and June 27, 1983.
Published/Created: Washington: U.S. G.P.O., 1984.
Description: vii, 775 p.: 1 map; 24 cm.
Notes: Distributed to some depository libraries in microfiche. "Serial no. J-98-34." Item 1042-A, 1042-B (microfiche) Includes bibliographical references.
Subjects: Prayer in the public schools--Law and legislation--United States.
Series: United States. Congress. Senate. S. hrg.; 98-1127.
Variant Series: S. hrg.; 98-1127
LC Classification: KF26 .J8359 1983h
Dewey Class No.: 344.73/0796 347.304796 19

United States. Congress. Senate. Committee on the Judiciary.
Proposed constitutional amendment to permit voluntary prayer: hearings before the Committee on the Judiciary, United States Senate, Ninety-seventh Congress, second session on S.J. Res. 199 ... July 29, Aug. 18, and Sept. 16, 1982.
Published/Created: Washington: U.S. G.P.O., 1982.
Description: v, 504 p.; 24 cm.
Notes: "Serial no. J-97-129." Item 1042-A, 1042-B (microfiche) Includes bibliographical references.
Subjects: Religion in the public schools--Law and legislation United States.
LC Classification: KF26 .J8 1982p
Dewey Class No.: 344.73/0796 347.304796 19

Warren, Rita.
God's champions / Rita Warren.
Edition Information: 1st ed.
Published/Created: McLean, Va.: Link Press, 1987.
Description: xii, 116 p., [12] p. of plates: ill. (some col.); 22 cm.
ISBN: 0912991062

Subjects: Warren, Rita. Prayer in the public schools--United States.
United States--Religion--1960- United States--Moral conditions.
LC Classification: BR1725.W327 A3 1987
Dewey Class No.: 277.3/0825 20

Warren, Rita.
   Mom, they won't let us pray ... / Rita Warren, with Dick Schneider.
Published/Created: [Chappaqua, N.Y.]: Chosen Books; Old Tappan,
N.J.: distributed by Revell, [1975]
Related Author: Schneider, Dick, 1922-
Description: 191 p.; 21 cm.
ISBN: 0912376104 :
Subjects: Warren, Rita. Prayer in the public schools--Massachusetts--
Brockton. Prayer in the public schools--United States.
LC Classification: LC113.B76 W37
Dewey Class No.: 377/.1

AUTHOR INDEX

A

Alley, Robert S., 51
Amos, Deborah, 64
Andryszewski, Tricia, 52

B

Barnard, Daniel D. (Daniel Dewey), 65
Barton, David, 52
Bedsole, Adolph, 53
Black, Hugo LaFayette, 53
Block, Herbert, 54

C

Church of Scotland, 55
Church of Scotland, 55
Citizens for God & Country (U.S.), 63
Columbia Broadcasting System, inc. CBS News, 70
Coniglio, John Vincent, 55
Cornish, Patty Jo, 55

D

Daum, Annette, 56
Dolbeare, Kenneth M., 56
Donovan, Marcella C., 56
Donovan, Teresa L., 56
Dudley, Mark E., 57
Duke, David W., 57
Durham, James R., 57
Dusek, Clare Lynn, 58

F

Feldman, Stephen M., 61
Fenwick, Lynda Beck, 58

G

Gay, Kathlyn, 59

H

Haas, Carol, 59
Hammond, Phillip E., 56

J

Jackson, Henry M. (Henry Martin), 67
Jaffa, Harry V., 58
Jones, Aubrey, 59

K

Keynes, Edward, 60
Kik, Jacob Marcellus, 60

L

Laubach, John Herbert, 60
Loren, Julia C., 61

M

Menendez, Albert J., 62
Miller, Randall K., 60
Muir, William Ker, 62
Murray, William J. (William Joseph), 62

N

National Back to God Movement, 64
National School Public Relations Association, 66
Neamon, Anne, 63, 64
Neuser, Wolfgang, 64
New Jersey. Legislature. Senate. Judiciary Committee, 65
New York (State). Legislature. Assembly. Committee on Colleges, Academies and Common Schools, 65

O

O'Hair, Madalyn Murray, 65
Ontario. Ministry of Education, 69

P

Piccione, Joseph, 56

R

Randolph, J. W., 66
Ravitch, Frank S., 66
Rice, Charles E., 67

S

Schneider, Dick, 73
Schwengel, Fred, 67, 68
Shedd, William Greenough Thayer, 68
Sikorski, Robert, 66
Smith, Rodney K., 69
Sorensen, Susan, 69
Stamp, Robert M., 69

T

Totenberg, Nina, 70

U

United States. Congress. House. Committee on the Judiciary. Subcommittee on the Constitution, 71
United States. Congress. Senate. Committee on the Judiciary, 71, 72
United States. Congress. Senate. Committee on the Judiciary. Subcommittee on Constitutional Amendments, 71
United States. Congress. Senate. Committee on the Judiciary. Subcommittee on the Constitution, 71, 72
United States. Congress. Senate. Committee on the Judiciary., 67

W

Warren, Rita, 72, 73
Whims, Joette, 69
Wylie, Chalmers, 67, 68

TITLE INDEX

A

A guide to the school prayer & religious liberty debate, 52
A moment of silence, 59
America's constitutional heritage--prayer and our public schools., 51
An outrageous idea: natural prayer, 55

B

Barnard's report on the use of the Bible in common schools., 65

C

Church and state: government and religion in the United States, 59

E

Emancipating school prayer, 58
Engel v. Vitale (1962): religion in the schools, 57
Engel v. Vitale: prayer in the public schools, 61
Engel v. Vitale: separation of church and state, 59

G

God's champions, 72

K

Kit Cat and the whirling watches: the story of a nation built by prayer, 69

L

Law and religion: a critical anthology, 61
Let us pray, 55
Let us pray: a plea for prayer in our schools, 62

M

Mom, they won't let us pray ..., 73

N

Neutral against God [sound recording]: school prayer and the First Amendment, 64

P

Papers of Hugo LaFayette Black, 1883-1976 (bulk 1926-1971), 53
Prayer and religion in public schools, 65
Prayer in public schools and the Constitution, 1961-1992, 66
Prayer in the public schools, 62
Principles of liberty: a practical guide to constitutional law, 57
Public prayer and the Constitution: a case study in constitutional interpretation, 69

R

Religion and the schools: from prayer to public aid., 66
Religious exercises in elementary and secondary schools, 69
Rumors of angels, 55

S

School prayer amendment debate. [Sound recording] , 67, 68
School prayer and discrimination: the civil rights of religious minorities and dissenters, 66
School prayer. Hearings, Eighty-ninth Congress, second session., 71
School prayer: a history of the debate, 52
School prayers, 60

Schulgottesdienst als sabbatliche Unterbrechung des Schulalltags, eine Chance für Schule und Kirche, 64
Secular darkness: religious right involvement in Texas public education, 1963-1989, 57
Should the children pray?: a historical, judicial, and political examination of public school prayer, 58
Storm over the Supreme Court. Part 2: The school prayer case [Motion picture], 69

T

The Court vs. Congress: prayer, busing, and abortion, 60
the Court, the Congress, and the First Amendment, 51
The school prayer decisions from court policy to local practice, 56
The Supreme Court and prayer in the public school., 60
The Supreme Court and public prayer, the need for restraint, 67
The Supreme Court and the '84 election [sound recording], 70
The Supreme Court decision on Bible reading and prayer, 53

V

Voluntary school prayer: judicial dilemma, proposed solutions, 56

W

Without a prayer: religious expression in public schools, 51

SUBJECT INDEX

A

Abington School District v. Schempp, 4, 5, 7, 9, 49
Abington, 4-10, 29, 36, 49
ACLU v. Blackhorse Pike Regional Board of Education, 44
Adler v. Duval County School Board, 44, 45
Aguillard, 21
Alabama, 10, 15, 16, 36, 38, 53
Amish, 26, 33
Arkansas, 19, 38

B

Bible reading, 3, 4, 8, 9, 10, 36, 42, 53
Bible, 3-5, 7-10, 27, 36, 38, 39, 42, 47, 53, 65
Bill of Rights, 6, 56, 64
Blackmun, Justice, 10, 15, 19, 20, 22, 24, 26
Board of Education of Westside Community Schools v. Mergens, 22, 31, 49
Boy Scouts, 47
Brennan, Justice, 19, 20, 22

Bronx Household of Faith v. Community School District No. 10, 47, 48
Burger, Chief Justice, 15, 16, 20, 21, 26

C

Campbell v. St. Tammany's School Board, 48
Chamberlin v. Dade County Board of Public Instruction, 9, 30
church, 16, 18, 21, 26, 33, 47, 57, 59, 61-64
Clear Creek policy, 44, 45
Clear Creek, 43, 44, 45
coercion, 7, 11, 13, 22, 45
Creationism Act, 20
creationism, 3, 18, 19, 38, 56

D

Declaration of Independence, 29, 30
devotional exercises, 2-4, 29, 36, 42
Doe v. Madison School District No. 321, 45
Douglas, Justice, 5, 17, 18, 26

E

education, 2, 4, 18, 25-27, 33, 37, 38, 40, 54, 57, 62
Edwards v. Aguillard, 19, 38
endorsement test, 13, 22, 45
Engel v. Vitale, 4-8, 57, 59, 61
Engel, 4-9, 27, 29, 36, 57, 59, 61, 70
Epperson v. Arkansas, 18, 19, 21, 27, 38, 49
Equal Access Act, 22, 28, 31
establishment clause, 2, 6-8, 11-13, 16, 19-24, 27-29, 31-33, 36-45, 49
evolution, 3, 18, 19, 38

F

First Amendment, 1, 2, 4, 5, 7-9, 12, 15, 16, 18, 19, 21, 23, 25, 27, 29, 31-33, 35, 36, 38, 40-42, 46, 48, 49, 53, 63, 64
flag salute, 25, 26
Florida, 10, 28, 41
football games, 2, 3, 13, 36, 45
Fortas, Justice, 18, 19
free exercise clause, 6-8, 21, 25, 26, 34
free speech clause, 3, 21, 23-25, 31, 32, 40, 41, 46, 48, 49
freedom of speech, 1, 3, 35, 48

G

Gideon Bible, 2, 40, 42
God, 5, 8, 10, 13, 30, 38, 63, 64, 72
graduation ceremonies, 2, 12, 30, 37, 43, 45
graduation ceremony, 10, 11, 12, 45

H

Harris, 45

I

information, iv
invocation, 10, 12, 13, 44, 45

J

Jehovah's Witnesses, 25
Joint School District No. 241 v. Harris, 44
Jones v. Clear Creek Independent School District, 43

K

Karen B. v. Treen, 10
Kennedy, Justice, 10, 22, 23, 24

L

Lamb's Chapel v. Center Moriches Free School District, 46
Lamb's Chapel v. Center Moriches Union Free School District, 11, 24, 34
Lamb's Chapel, 11, 24, 25, 34, 46, 47
Lee v. Weisman, 10, 11, 14, 37, 43, 45
Lemon test, 6, 7, 11, 13, 16, 22, 45
Lord's Prayer, 5
Louisiana, 10, 19, 38, 48

M

March v. Chambers, supra, 12
Marsh, 12
McCollum v. Board of Education, 17, 18, 21, 39
Mergens, 22, 23, 24, 31
moment of silence, 15, 16, 29, 37, 45, 65
moments of silence, 3, 35, 37, 42
'monkey law', 19
Murray v. Curlett, 5

Murray, 5, 9, 62, 65

N

New York, 3, 4, 7, 17, 30, 46, 47, 55-57, 61-63, 65-68
noncurricular religious expression, 21
nonsectarian, 10, 11, 13, 37, 43, 44, 46

O

O'Connor, Justice, 10, 15, 19, 21-24, 49

P

Pledge of Allegiance, 3, 25, 26, 29, 30
prayer, 2-16, 28, 29, 36, 37, 42-45, 48, 51-53, 56, 58-64, 66-72
private religious groups, 17, 35
private religious speech, 3, 4
public schools, 1-4, 7, 10, 11, 16-18, 21, 22, 26, 28-30, 32-37, 39, 41, 42, 48, 49, 51-73

R

Rehnquist, Chief Justice, 10, 12, 14-16, 20-24, 26
"released time" program, 17
religious attire, 40, 41, 42
religious expression, 2-4, 7, 21, 26, 28, 29, 34-36, 42, 49, 51
religious instruction, 2-4, 17, 18, 28, 35, 39, 42, 47
religious worship, 21, 31, 42, 46, 47
Rosenberger v. Rector and Visitors of the University of Virginia, 23
Rosenberger, 11, 23, 24, 31

S

Santa Fe Independent School District v. Doe, 7, 11, 13, 28, 37, 44, 45
Santa Fe, 7, 11, 13, 28, 37, 44, 45
Scalia, Justice, 10, 12-14, 20, 22, 23, 24
school curriculum, 2, 27, 38
school day, 2, 4, 5, 9, 10, 15, 17, 28, 29, 35, 37, 39, 42
school prayer, 64
secularism, 9
Souter, Justice, 10, 23, 24
Stevens, Justice, 10, 13, 15, 19, 20-24
Stewart, Justice, 5, 8, 9
Stone v. Graham, 20, 27, 40
Stone, 20, 21, 25, 27, 40
strict neutrality, 5, 49
student-initiated religious groups, 2, 3, 35

T

Ten Commandments, 2, 20, 21, 27, 40
The Good News Club v. Milford Central School, 47
Thomas, Justice, 10, 12, 14, 23, 24

V

voluntary prayer, 15, 16, 29, 37

W

Wallace v. Jaffree, 10, 15, 28, 37
Wallace, 10, 15, 16, 28, 36, 37
Weisman, 10, 43
West Virginia State Board of Education v. Barnette, 25, 30
West Virginia, 25, 30, 37
White, Justice, 5, 10, 12, 15, 16, 18-22, 24, 26, 53
Widmar v. Vincent, 21, 31

Widmar, 21, 22, 24, 31
Wisconsin v. Yoder, 26, 33
World War II, 25

Z

Zorach v. Clauson, 17
Zorach, 17, 21, 28